JAPAN:
Economic Growth, Resource Scarcity, and Environmental Constraints

Westview Replica Editions

This book is a Westview Replica Edition. The concept of
Replica Editions is a response to the crisis in academic and
informational publishing. Library budgets for books have been
severely curtailed; economic pressures on the university presses
and the few private publishing companies primarily interested in
scholarly manuscripts have severely limited the capacity of the
industry to properly serve the academic and research communities.
Many manuscripts dealing with important subjects, often repre-
senting the highest level of scholarship, are today not economically viable publishing projects. Or, if they are accepted for
publication, they are often subject to lead times ranging from
one to three years. Scholars are understandably frustrated when
they realize that their first-class research cannot be published
within a reasonable time frame, if at all.

Westview Replica Editions seem to us one feasible and prac-
tical solution to the crisis. The concept is simple. We accept
a manuscript in camera-ready form and move it immediately into
the production process. The responsibility for textual and copy
editing lies with the author or sponsoring organization. If
necessary we will advise the author on proper preparation of
footnotes and bibliography. The manuscript is acceptable as
typed for a thesis or dissertation or prepared in any other
clearly organized and readable way, though we prefer it typed
according to our specifications. The end result is a book produced by lithography and bound in hard covers. Edition sizes
range from 200 to 600 copies. We will include among Westview
Replica Editions only works of outstanding scholarly quality or
of great informational value, and we will exercise our usual
editorial standards and quality control.

Japan: Economic Growth, Resource Scarcity,
and Environmental Constraints
Edward A. Olsen

This study evaluates, from a neo-Malthusian perspective,
Japan's current status and its prognosis in the context of the
country's economic vulnerabilities. Drawing on the theoretical
contributions of Malthus, N. Georgescu-Roegen, H. and M.
Sprout, and assorted environmental-ecological doomsayers, the
author reaches pessimistic conclusions about Japan's very long
term prospects, but holds out some slim hope for Japan if
international cooperation of nearly utopian dimensions can be
achieved.

Edward A. Olsen, research analyst at the U.S. Department of
State, received his doctorate from American University's
School of International Service. He previously served as pro-
fessor of political science at George Williams College.

JAPAN:
Economic Growth, Resource Scarcity, and Environmental Constraints

Edward A. Olsen

Westview Press
Boulder, Colorado

A Westview Replica Edition

Published in 1978 in the United States of America by

Westview Press, Inc.
5500 Central Avenue
Boulder, Colorado 80301
Frederick A. Praeger, Publisher and Editorial Director

Library of Congress Number: 77-28013
ISBN: 0-89158-064-6

Printed and bound in the United States of America

CONTENTS

TABLES

PREFACE

The majority of this study was drawn from the author's dissertation research (Ph.D., May 1974, School of International Service, The American University). Many scholars directly and indirectly contributed to the ideas incorporated in that original research. However, I particularly wish to express my gratitude to the members of my dissertation committee for their informal comments and insights and to those colleagues who offered helpful advice with the current revision.

The present study also has substantial portions which were not part of the original study. These additions largely were written while I was an Assistant Professor of Political Science at George Williams College in Downers Grove, Illinois. A small amount of subsequent revision -- required to update statistics and bring textual references to contemporary events up to date -- were made while I was a research analyst with the U.S. Department of State (INR). These final revisions were made independently and without recourse to official sources of information available to me. Consequently the views expressed in this study are solely those of the author.

Chapter 1
INTRODUCTION

The predecessor of this study was originally prepared as a doctoral dissertation in International Studies with a more broadly based theoretical and regional focus. Entitled "East Asia and the ecological perspective on the roots of power of H. & M. Sprout: an inquiry into the nature of power and the power of nature in East Asian political cultures," the original study sought to reassess the theoretical contributions of Professors Harold and Margaret Sprout of Princeton University by applying those theories in the regional context of East Asia: China, Japan, and Korea.

The present study differs from its parent in its emphasis. It draws less specifically on the Sprouts' work and focuses exclusively on Japan. The theoretical assumptions implicit in this study -- while drawing upon the work of the Sprouts[1] and others working in their field -- are decidedly more Malthusian than the Sprouts. Specifically, and from the standpoint of economic theory, this study owes a fundamental debt to Professor Nicholas Georgescu-Roegens' work on the role of thermodynamic entropy in economic systems. In addition, this study was

1

consciously drafted in strongly neo-Malthusian terms.
Using these neo-Malthusian assumptions an attempt is
made to assess Japan's economic vulnerability and
its impact on Japan as a force in world politics.

Based, as it is, on a controversial set of
pessimistic assumptions this study draws tentative
conclusions with which many will disagree. I recognize the possible validity of opposing viewpoints
given the validity of opposing assumptions -- what
the Sprouts have termed the "engineering perspective," e.g. all problems have solutions.[2] However,
I deny the validity of those assumptions. Instead,
I prefer to see problems as Santayana saw them:

> All problems are divided into two classes:
> soluble questions, which are trivial, and
> important questions, which are insoluble.

I contend the neo-Malthusian problems which Japan
and the world confront are in fact overwhelmingly
important and probably insoluble in terms of a
comprehensive solution.

Seeking a solution, humanity on a finite world
is forced to face the inescapable facts of the
earth's carrying capacity. Carrying capacity is not
a question of nature controlling man, but of nature
imposing limitations on man's endeavors. The difficulty with this notion is that "limitation" can be
conceived too rigidly. Many economists who criticize
neo-Malthusian analysis fall into this trap. A more
desirable notion of carrying capacity is that of
flexible limits. Such a notion may seem inherently
contradictory. To clarify this seeming contradiction
we must recall that the idea of "nature" is a
cultural phenomenon and that any limits which we

2

consider to be imposed by nature are, therefore, always relative to the goals posited by cultural man. Thus the limits are flexible in the sense that they are determined by and respond to man's goals. While the limit must be considered a flexible limit, it is a limit nonetheless.

In short, the place of natural resources, renewable and non-renewable, in the ecumene is not determining but they are delimiting. A shortage of resources will not necessarily be catastrophic if managed wisely, but with poor economic and political management shortages can range from depressive to utter catastrophe.

Economists commonly attack the notion of exponential growth leading to eventual disaster by claiming the constraining limits are not fixed, but are also exponential. They thereby demonstrate an unfortunate lack of comprehension of the ecological paradigm. They are correct that limits are not fixed, but are in error when they transform what are actually flexible limits bound by earthly constraints into exponentially growing limits. Limits can be reconstructed by man according to his goals, but finity can not be transformed into infinity by assumption.

The neo-Malthusian contention of this study is that the pressures of growth in the context of flexible limits will become too great for compensation or substitution and that new approaches will have to be developed to handle the dilemma. In other words, the problem is the probable failure of economic adjustment mechanisms -- the inability of the world economy in a future Malthusian crisis to

internalize disruptive externalities. The economic
systems can not provide answers because "answers" do
not exist for this question.

The great majority of economists are highly
critical of Malthusian economic analysis. A notable
exception to this rule is the insightful work of
Professor Nicholas Georgescu-Roegen of Vanderbilt
University. Before turning to an examination of
Japan, it is worthwhile briefly examining some key
elements in Georgescu-Roegen's neo-Malthusian
economic analysis which, along with the better known
theoretical contributions of Malthus himself and of
Harold and Margaret Sprout, underlies this study.[3]

Georgescu-Roegen denounces the affinity for
mechanistic dogma demonstrated by most economists.
He charges that their attachment to equilibrium
theory has led standard economists to ignore or play
down systemic feedback mechanisms, generally treat-
ing feedback in terms of maintaining equilibrium and
not in evolutionary terms.

Seeking to move away from a mechanical model
in economics, Georgescu-Roegen argues for the
applicability to economics of the Second Law of
Thermodynamics -- the Entropy Law. A highly complex
concept in physics, entropy amounts to an "index of
the amount of unavailable energy in a given thermodynamic system at a given moment of its evolution."
In broader terms, entropy is an index of irrevocable
dissipation of energy and -- by extension -- of
matter. Georgescu-Roegen contends that in essence
thermodynamics constitutes "a physics of economic
value". Supporting a shift in models he argues that
"the economy of any life process is governed, not

4

by the laws of mechanics, but by the Entropy Law."
Central to the importance of this conceptual shift
is the fact that "the Entropy Law is the taproot of
economic scarcity." In a hypothetical purely mechanical world energy could be used over and over again,
equipment and organisms would never wear out, and
there would never be a scarcity of energy or
materials.

In a sense economists begin to deal with the
reality of economic scarcity in the oft-repeated
phrase "there is no such thing as a free lunch."
However, they generally miss the point because they
address this notion in terms of price and cost. In
contrast to this simple perspective, Georgescu-
Roegen charges "To believe that this equality also
prevails in terms of entropy constitutes one of the
most dangerous economic myths. In the context of
entropy, --- , any process in nature must result in
a deficit for the entire system."

Though Malthus and a variety of later neo-
Malthusian environmentalists perceived the general
outline of trends enforced by the Entropy Law
acting on social-economic systems, they often
reached erroneous conclusions. A basic and often
noted error involves their timing. Malthus and his
followers looked for a doomsday on the horizon,
frequently speculating incorrectly as to its
imminence and with insufficient regard to the
social adaptability of human cultures. A specific
timetable for Malthusian disaster is probably
impossible to forecast since the social and natural
variables are too numerous and the forecast itself
may influence the course of events. Nor is such a

disaster likely to occur in one fell swoop. As
Georgescu-Roegen correctly observes, when and if the
"end" comes it will likely be gradual, following "a
very long series of surreptitious, protracted
crises."

More importantly, Georgescu-Roegen uncovered a
vital flaw in Malthus' theory and in the major
modern analyses of a neo-Malthusian bent (notably
The Limits to Growth and "Blueprint for Survival"[4]).
As Georgescu-Roegen insightfully observes, Malthus
and many of his adherents "were set exclusively on
proving the impossibility of growth." As a consequence "they were easily deluded by a simple, now
widespread, but false syllogism: since exponential
growth in a finite world leads to disaster of all
kinds, ecological salvation lies in the stationary
state." Georgescu-Roegen is a post-Malthusian
theoretician in that he is more Malthusian than
Malthus. Based on the correct observation that a
stationary state global economy will also sooner or
later collapse, Georgescu-Roegen concludes "the
most desirable state is not a stationary, but a
declining one," but also cautions that it is
unlikely that anyone will ever produce a "blueprint
for the ecological salvation of the human species."

Malthusian concepts are critical for the
future of man on earth.[5] The fact that man can
stretch constraining limits does not mean that
those limits can be made to vanish. Malthusian
flexible limits are more likely to flex to meet our
demands by assuming their validity and acting upon
that assumption than by ridiculing Malthus. Yet
uninformed ridicule remains pervasive. How long

this condition will persist is an open question.

Japan is not unique in confronting the Malthusian dilemma. Other countries -- notably those of Western Europe -- confront the dilemma in similar ways. However, for reasons examined in the body of this study, the Japanese situation is potentially far more acute than the circumstances of other advanced industrialized states. It may therefore provide an instructive example.

NOTES

1. Sprout, Harold H., "Political Geography as a Political Science field" in American Political Science Review, May 1931, pp. 439-442.

Sprout, Harold and Margaret, "Geography and international politics in an era of revolutionary change" in Journal of Conflict Resolution, Vol. 4, March 1960, pp. 145-161.

------, The Ecological Perspective on Human Affairs with Special Reference to International Politics (Princeton, 1965).

------, An Ecological Paradigm for the Study of International Politics, (Princeton, 1968).

------, "The dilemma of rising demands and insufficient resources" in World Politics, July 1968, pp. 660-693.

------, "Environmental factors in the study of international politics" in James N. Rosenau (ed.), International Politics and Foreign Policy (New York, 1969).

------, Ecology and Politics in America: Some Issues and Alternatives, (Morristown, 1971).

------, "The ecological viewpoint - and others"

in Cyril E. Black and Richard A. Falk (eds.), <u>The Future of the International Legal Order, Volume IV: The Structure of the International Environment</u>, (Princeton, 1972).

------, <u>Toward a Politics of the Planet Earth</u>, (New York, 1971).

------, "National priorities: demands, resources, dilemmas" in <u>World Politics</u>, January 1972, pp. 293-317.

------, "Environmental politics: what role for political scientists?" in Stuart S. Nagel (ed.), <u>Environmental Politics</u>, (New York, 1974).

2. Sprouts, <u>Toward a Politics of the Planet Earth</u>, op. cit., pp. 17-18.

3. The most comprehensive statement of Georgescu-Roegen's views can be found in his <u>The Entropy Law and the Economic Process</u>, (Cambridge, 1971). The best summary of his views is his "Energy and Economic myths" in <u>Southern Economic Journal</u>, January 1975, pp. 347-381. The quoted portions in the following text are from pp. 351-355 and 366-369 of the latter article.

4. Dennis L. Meadows, Donella H. Meadows, Jørgen Randers, and William W. Behrens III, <u>The Limits to Growth</u>, (New York, 1972).

"Blueprint for survival" in <u>Ecologist</u>, January 1972, pp. 1-43.

5. The term "Malthusian" is frequently used throughout this study in a broad sense to indicate a generic perspective.

Chapter 2

JAPANESE ECONOMIC GROWTH, AN OVERVIEW

Japan's economic growth in the post World War
Two era is one of the marvels of the Twentieth
Century. Out of the ashes of defeat the Japanese
phoenix arose and attained undreamt of glories.
Japan is the first Asian nation to rank among the
leading economies of the modern world. It reached
this position on the basis of a market economy,
although one with important differences from other
advanced economies. By 1968 -- one hundred years
after the Meiji restoration put Japan on the path
to modernity -- Japan's output of goods and
services exceeded that of West Germany. Its economy
became the third largest in the world after that of
the United States and the Soviet Union.

There are two overwhelmingly significant
features of Japan's post-1868 modernization.
Unfortunately, neither are widely recognized outside
Japan:

Common beliefs about Japan's modernization
posit a quaintly primitive Japan being massively
changed by a sudden influx of notions and habits
derived from vastly different Western cultures.
There is, of course, an element of truth in such

beliefs, but not a dominant element. Japan's modernization and industrialization after 1868 did not
signify a sharp break with its past, but rather, in
Sir George Sansom's phrase, "only a gathering of
speed."[1] Japan already was well on its way toward
a changed future when the upheavals of the nineteenth century intervened. The indigenous trend
toward modernization most assuredly owed a debt to
the limited Western influences permitted by the
Tokugawa Shogunate, but this trend owed much more
to the character of Japanese social institutions --
particularly commercial institutions -- which were
markedly similar to those which prevailed in Europe
as it developed. Japanese society was more attuned
to the development of modern capitalism than were
other Asian societies.[2]

     Japan's economy expanded quite steadily except
for the devastation wrought by the Second World War.
Japan's postwar economic development was heavily
influenced by Japan's ties to the United States.
However, frequently made assumptions that the United
States was responsible for that development are
unwarranted. The United States was the catalyst,
but the spirit behind the recovery and expansion
of Japan's postwar economy was Japanese. The outer
facade of occupation induced economic reforms
dissolved with renewed independence. After that the
Japanese regained their own momentum. That momentum
has been pushing Japan forward since the mid-1950s.

     Japan's position in the world economy was
achieved by a phenomenally high and sustained
growth rate that is unmatched by any other major
economy. Postwar rebuilding of the economy was

10

largely complete by 1954 when the pre-war 1939 level
of peak per capita income was reattained. At that
point the Japanese economy "took off" at an
astounding pace:

Table 2.1

AVERAGE ANNUAL INCREASE IN GNP AT CONSTANT PRICES

	1950-60	1960-70
Japan	9.1%	11.3%
West Germany	7.9	4.7
France	4.5	5.6
United Kingdom	2.8	2.7
Italy	5.6	5.7
United States	3.2	4.2

Source: OECD

Japan's remarkable economic achievement was the
product of several factors which permitted it to
overcome handicaps of limited size (approximately
that of California with only fifteen percent of its
land area arable), a disproportionately large
population, and a severe lack of the natural
resources requisite for industrial growth. Leading
the list of Japan's assets are its extraordinarily
skilled, ambitious, and resourceful people who
devised the social mechanisms enabling Japan to
surmount its handicaps. Drawing upon an entrenched
"protestant" work ethic, the Japanese have:
-- Maintained very high levels of investment,
   unparalleled in the West, which were spurred by
   high domestic savings rates. Such savings were
   achieved as a result of Japanese frugality and
   its semi-annual lump payment system which
   fosters personal savings;

11

-- Effectively utilized their highly literate, well
   trained, and diligent labor force which approached
   the task of economic nation-building with scant
   regard for personal benefit while striving for
   the national good;
-- Strengthened the competitive skills of its able
   managerial class within the paternalistic, com-
   placent, and generally strike-free milieu of
   Japanese labor-management relations;
-- Successfully drawn upon pre-tested foreign
   technological imports, thereby benefitting from
   modern systems of production with little of the
   risks or costs of their development;
-- Kept their expenditures for defense and social
   overhead to a minimum via the security treaty
   with the United States and, until recently, the
   forbearance of a compliant Japanese public
   willing to do without for the present in exchange
   for long range benefits. Funds shifted from these
   purposes contributed to growth in other areas;
   and
-- Viewed government assistance in capitalist
   planning as an asset rather than interference.
   The Japanese view government-corporate interaction as a forum for achieving consensus on
   growth plans. The extraordinary levels of back-
   scratching in Japan would be anathema in Western
   societies attuned to the give and take of more
   hostile competitive relationships between the
   public and private sectors. However, with the
   knowledge that all parties work toward the same
   end, the Japanese have readily accepted the
   hand-in-glove relationship in which the government offered financial incentives in foreign

exchange allocations through the early 1960s,
guarantees of industrial credit, and -- until the
late 1960s -- protection against competition from
foreign capital and imports. Despite occasional
scandals, the Japanese remain committed to their
system.

If one is to believe the estimate of Herman
Kahn, the Japanese economic system will continue to
expand relentlessly until, in the next century, the
world will be oriented toward Japan.[3] One must take
his predictions, along with those of other
unrestrained optimists, with a grain of salt and
bear in mind Mark Twain's comments on extrapolation
and the pitfalls of "science."[4] Despite such overt
optimism, even the more moderate observers of
Japan's economy contend that it will continue to
expand for the indefinite future -- albeit at a more
moderate rate. Even at such rates Japan's per capita
income in the 1980s is likely to be approximately
eight thousand dollars per year or about the same
as that anticipated for the United States at that
time.

Data on Japan's economic growth are important
in two major respects. Firstly, they reflect a
growing economy. Secondly, the frequency with which
such data are mentioned in Japan and abroad reflects
the Japanese preoccupation with growth. As Kahn
correctly observed, the Japanese "watch growth rates
the way Americans watch baseball standings or foot-
ball scores."[5] This comparison is instructive in
ways not intended by Kahn. As in sports, the
Japanese public's interest in growth rate scores
has had a detached sense of unreality about it.

It has been as though the scores were unrelated to their personal lives and were merely the affair of some remote and abstract "team" of which they were a supporter. Until fairly recently the Japanese seldom gave any thought to their intimate membership in the team. They would actively cheer on the team's local farm club (e.g., their employer), but did not consider the overall score to be directly related to their personal well being.

Two related topics served in recent years to refocus the attention of the Japanese on the scores and what they imply for their lives. The first is the notion of the Japanese as "economic animals." This widely used expression gave the Japanese reason to pause. They dislike the phrase because of its tinges of racism derived from the use of the term "animal"[6] and because of what it says about the single-minded character of their society. Whether the Japanese are, in fact, "economic animals" which inhabit Japan, Inc." remains a controversial question. Leading authorities can be found on both sides of the issue. This question will not be resolved here, but it is well to note in passing that the Japanese do not appear to be "economic animals" any more than equally aggressive North Americans or Western Europeans. To a large degree the faults which are encompassed by this phrase are common to all advanced economies.

The second topic is the reexamination of the purposes of growth which has of late become a pre-occupation for many Japanese. By the late 1960s the Japanese began to introspectively ask themselves why they want their economy to grow or, indeed, if they want it to grow. Attention in Japan has focused more on the question of "why" rather than "if". However, even this is a vast improvement over the condition which prevailed previously of docile acceptance of tacit assumptions that growth is good. Japanese awareness of the difficulties accruing from rapid and sometimes unwise economic growth was belated. It was not until the dangers of kōgai (environmental hazards) became too apparent to deny and other peoples, who were suffering from similar societal maladies, began to point their collective fingers at Japan that the Japanese en masse awoke to the problems confronting them. The Japanese were late-comers. Prior to the late 1960s Japan's primary fear related to economic growth was that they might once more fall into the trap of building an economy based on war materiel. In this context, Ronald Dore correctly observed that "economic growth can sometimes be bought at a higher price than it is worth."[7] Although the context has changed to the environment, the truth of that statement is not diminished.

Japan's immediate concern arising from rapid economic growth was social devastation caused by kōgai. Japanese industry is highly concentrated in relatively narrow coastal bands. The gross pollution of its smelting, paper pulp, and petro-chemical sectors caused the proliferation of pollution related diseases such as the now infamous Minamata and Itai-itai (ouch-ouch) maladies. A vocal movement of environmentalists emerged in Japan in response to the diseases and has achieved moderate success.

Japan's rapid economic growth also caused public concern in more traditional economic realms.

15

Japan's genrally docile people, through the medium
of protest votes for radical opposition party
candidates, called for increased expenditures on
neglected areas of social overhead. Housing, social
security, health and welfare, urbanization and its
problems of transport, sanitation, and recreation
were all pressed by social activists. The long
awaited future promised by generations of Japanese
planners was demanded with greater urgency. While
some success was achieved in these areas, the
Japanese still lag far behind other advanced
economies in terms of the material quality of life
they experience. Given the physically narrow
confines with which they must contend, it is
doubtful that the Japanese can ever approach the
spatial qualities of Western material cultures.
Although they occasionally display envy of such
Western attributes, Japanese cultural adaptations
to their confined material milieu will probably
enable them to devise their own version of the "good
life."

Other areas of economic distress caused, in
part, by rapid economic growth have also been met
with some success. The rate of price inflation
reached a peak in 1973. A mixed consequence of
rising foreign commodity prices, the pressures of
mounting economic and social demands in an urbanizing state, increases in distribution costs, and
largely untrammeled economic growth, inflation was
fought with varied success. Complicating this fight
was the downturn in the export-import imbalance as
a result of the mid-1973 downward revaluation of
the yen, accompanied by measures liberalizing
imports and foreign investments in Japan. The

16

embarassingly large foreign exchange reserves
accumulated during the years 1970-1973 had been
viewed as a problem of excessively rapid economic
growth also -- the result of a surge in exports
which was unmatched by imports. However, this
temporary problem was resolved partly by policy
dictate but also by necessity as the prices of
commodity imports inflated and recession hit Japan
and the international economy.

These and other emergent problems of Japan's
economic growth are probably manageable in the
short run. With the benefit of great foresight,
skillful planning, and adroit management which the
Japanese have frequently demonstrated, the Japanese
will probably be able to cope with their immediate
problems. The very long run is another matter.

Commodity price increases resulting from
foreign political manipulation have, to date, been
met by Japanese accomodation. As long as these
mechanisms of the international economy remain
operational, the Japanese will grit their teeth
and bear the pressures. However, domestic societal
pressures stemming from the encroachment of kogai
amid a hectic and competitive life style may
detrimentally influence the social fabric of Japan
which has supported the Japanese economic miracle.
If these forces tear the fabric, how will Japan
bear economic pressures?

A question of great importance facing Japan
and its interdependent partners in the international
economy is how Japan views the prospect of possible
increased neo-Malthusian economic pressures on the
world economy. Now that more than three postwar

decades have passed the reemergence of Japanese
economic strength increasingly is accepted as a
legitimate basis for Japan's renewed international
political recognition. Is this acceptance warranted?
Is Japan truly a great economic power? The contention
of this study is that, while Japan is an economic
giant, it is a giant with terribly vulnerable feet
of clay.

Were Japan merely a small and insignificant
island nation in the far reaches of the Pacific,
their growth related attitudes and international
policies would not overly concern anyone else. On
the contrary, the Japanese -- occupying a major
portion of the world economy -- hold views and have
national interests which should be thoroughly
understood abroad, but which are not. If it is true
that when the economy of the United States catches
cold the capitalist world gets pneumonia, is it any
less true that a critical illness of the dynamic
Japanese economy holds the potential for withering
the sinews of the international economy? This study
contends that the Japanese economy may well become
critically "ill" as its societal ability to adapt
to emerging neo-Malthusian forces of commodity
power is stretched to the limits.[8]

What the Japanese think and do about growth
and the prospects for a Malthusian world are of
great importance to the entire world. The importance
is continually enlarging as Japan's place in the
world's economy becomes more central. Sir Halford
Mackinder -- the noted British geopolitical
theorist -- postulated the existence of a Eurasian
heartland of immense indigenous natural wealth

18

which held the potential for world rule. This study
contends the world has not yet given enough critical
thought to the possible negative role of a country
such as Japan in a future world of Malthusian
dimensions -- Japan as a vacuous "heartland." This
is a serious omission. In order to help rectify
this omission, we shall examine in the following
three sections the changing set of beliefs under-
girding Japanese economic prowess, the issue of
Japan as a neo-Malthusian state, and Japan's options
in its international relations within the context
of neo-Malthusian pressures.

NOTES

1. Sansom, George B., The Western World and Japan,
a Study in the Interaction of European and Asiatic
Cultures (New York, 1950), p. 223.
2. For further comments on Japan's greater receptiv-
ity to modern capitalism, see: Joseph Needham, The
Grand Titration; Science & Society in East and West
(Toronto, 1969), p. 206; and Norman Jacobs, The
Origins of Modern Capitalism and Eastern Asia (Hong
Kong, 1958).

3. Kahn, Herman. The Emerging Japanese Superstate
(Englewood Cliffs, 1970), p. 2.

4. Twain said of science: "In the space of 176 years
the Lower Mississippi has shortened itself 242 miles.
That is an average of a trifle over one mile and a
third per year. Therefore, any calm person, who is
not blind or idiotic, can see that in the old
oolitic Silurian period, just a million years ago
next November, the Lower Mississippi River was
upwards on one million three hundred thousand miles

long, and stuck out over the Gulf of Mexico like a
fishing rod. And by the same token any person can
see that 742 years from now the Lower Mississippi
will be only a mile and three-quarters long, and
Cairo and New Orleans will have joined their streets
together, and be plodding comfortably along under a
single mayor.... There is something fascinating
about science. One gets such wholesome returns of
conjecture out of such a trifling investment in
fact."

5. Kahn, op. cit., p. 113.

6. For a discussion of their dislike see: Gregory
Clark, "The fragile face of force" in Survival,
March 1970, pp. 85-87.

7. Dore, Ronald P., "Japan as a model of economic
development" in Archives européennes de sociologie,
No. 1, 1964, p. 154.

8. All references to "limits" in this study are to
be considered in the context of flexible limits as
outlined in the introduction.

Chapter 3
CHANGING JAPANESE PERCEPTIONS OF NATURE
AND SOCIETAL CONSTRAINTS

In order to move from a discussion of Japan's
economic growth to an evaluation of the Malthusian
problems Japan may confront in the future we must
first pause to consider the set of attitudes the
Japanese bring to bear on the issue. Since economic
growth is a product of cultural interaction with
natural support systems, we will seek to evaluate
the ways the Japanese view nature, how they norma-
tively interpret economic growth as a social good,
and how their perceptions are being altered by the
conflicting pressures of modernity vs. traditionalism.

TRADITIONAL JAPANESE VIEWS OF NATURE

Japan is in many respects an offspring of the
Chinese cultural tradition. It is significant that
Japan's first major infusion of Sinic culture came
during China's T'ang dynasty (618-906 A.D.), a
period when Chinese concerns with nature were at a
critically formative stage. The Japanese, by adapt-
ing T'ang China's culture to their own indigenous
culture, were fortunate in their timing. Had the
Japanese discovered China at an earlier period, they

might well have absorbed traditions which would have been antagonistic to their indigenous culture. It is to this indigenous culture to which we shall turn first.

The early Japanese way of life centered around a vague system of beliefs concerning man as an integral part of nature. In fact, man was such an integral part of his surroundings that there was not any word for "nature." The concept of nature as something apart from man had not yet developed. Shintō is the name that became applied to these vague beliefs. At first the name, Shintō, did not exist either. It is a Sinicized term which came into being at a later date so that its adherents could compare their beliefs with the religions imported from China. Early Shintō was not really a religion. A religion can be defined, but early Shintō defies any clear-cut definition. Rather, it was an intuitive feeling which pervaded a primitive and superstitious society. This feeling linked man as one with his surroundings and made him observant of the sensibilities of those surroundings whether animate or inanimate. This intuitive and emotional relationship is something which has appeared in other cultures -- for example, in cultures as diverse as the early Greeks and the American Indians. It is also a state of mind which has been advocated by many contemporary conservation activists. A unique aspect of this state of mind of early Japan is that it has never been totally displaced in the Japanese psyche. Despite the changes which have occured in Japan in a span of some centuries, a strain of primitive folk Shintō remains to this day in the make-up of the Japanese.

Shintō as a religion did not remain on this primeval level for long after the influx of Chinese culture. Over the years it developed into a more highly structured set of doctrines. Despite the superstructure it developed as state-Shintō in the post-Meiji period (1868-1945), there remained within Shintō one aspect which retained the essence of its original form. This is the continued belief in resident spirits -- kami -- in the natural environment. Muraoka termed this element meijo shugi (brightness-purityism).[1] This aspect of organized Shintō in conjunction with the Chinese concepts of man in nature harmony as influenced by the Taoists, which were imported during the T'ang dynasty, found a receptive home in Japanese culture. This amalgam of man in nature views persisted in Japan up until the impact of the West. However, as Japanese culture was further Sinified, Confucian notions of a man-centered world view grew in prominence.

Despite, or perhaps because of, this overall trend, Japanese culture developed a sense of wistfulness toward its past. This occured in China as well, but for the Chinese the focus was on past greatness, while for the Japanese the focus was on the primitive and austere. In the immediately pre-modern era in Japan we find examples of such notions among both Confucians and Shintōists. Two exceptional neo-Confucianists of eighteenth century Japan, Kaibara Ekken and Miura Baien, broke away from Confucian concerns with man's central place and sought to propogate a view of man integrated with and filial to nature in the sense that man owed a debt to nature which he must repay with careful devotion.[2] Neither of these figures represent a dominant influence, but they -- along with Shintōists such as the somewhat later agrarian reformer Ninomiya Sontoku -- kept intellectually alive the fundamentals of early Japanese beliefs. Ninomiya left the following poem for posterity:

> The beaten path
> Is covered with fallen leaves;
> Brush them aside
> And see the footprints
> Of the Sun-goddess. [3]

This expresses very graphically the latent essence of Japanese culture which lay beneath the Sinic overlay.

The modernization of Japan in the nineteenth century did little to uncover this essence. Instead, another layer imported from the West was placed upon the cultural amalgam which is Japan. Just as China had attempted to reject Western culture while accepting Western science and technology, Japan sought these same goals under the slogan of "Eastern ethics and Western science." Unlike the Chinese who futilely wrestled with this issue for many years, the Japanese quite rapidly recognized that Western culture and science were very much a unitary phenomenon and that to accept the one meant acceptance of at least a portion of the other. It was not until the turn of the century and the early twentieth century that revisionism set in once more and the Japanese longingly turned to their distant past. In the intervening years it was Western culture with its science in the forefront which set the pace for Japan.

After the turn of the century the Japanese grew increasingly dissatisfied with the excesses of hyperbolic converts to Western cultures. Their reaction was to reexamine their past. In the face of this perceived threat to their ancient if under-used traditions the Japanese placed new value on those traditions. It is interesting to note that the word we now use to describe these renewed interests -- their aesthetic drives -- was not known to pre-modern Japanese. It is a term (bigaku) which was devised about 1880 by Japanese seeking to assess the glories of the West then in vogue.[4] The irony is that this Western introduced concept was used as a means to comprehend the essence of Japan's past. This essence -- "the footprints of the Sun-goddess" -- was still there beneath the layers of Sinic and Western leaves.

The essence of the old ways remained in the life styles of the rural population living close to the land. It remained also in the arts which traced their roots to rural Japan. For it was rural Japan, where the people remained intimate with the spirits of their natural environment, which was the living repository of Japan's cultural essence. Japanese closeness to nature was similar to the notions of the more metaphysical Taoists, but differed in the sense that Taoists consciously sought unity with an idealized nature, while the Japanese intuited the essence of nature. In seeking to return to the intuitive old ways the Japanese were reacting against the secular materialism of life; against what Akutagawa Ryūnosuke's Kappa character,"Lap," termed the most important religion of Japan -- "modernism, or life-worship."[5]

25

NATURE IN CONTEMPORARY JAPAN

In contemporary Japan traditional Japanese
attitudes toward nature remain viable despite the
pressures they have withstood. Shintō remains alive
if not particularly robust. In Japan's urbanizing
society the Shintō ceremony has devolved into a
somewhat anachronistic rite performed more to
placate the human psyche than the natural spirits.
The standard bearers of the old traditions survive,
but frequently are human relics euphamistically
called "human treasures."

The changes which have occured in the short
span of years since the end of the Second World War
make the pre-war standards which were criticized as
excessively materialistic seem very traditional by
comparison. Thus when the Japanese solitary holdout
on Guam, Sergeant Yokoi Shōichi, returned to Japan
after an absence of twenty eight years and
expressed a desire to return to a mountain near his
birthplace and pay his respects,[6] the Japanese
public respected his wishes but thought them a bit
quaint. The fact that Yokoi, a man who probably
considered himself to be "modern" when he left
Japan as a young man, was now considered a quaint
oddity says a great deal about the changes which
have occured in postwar Japan and how those changes
have influenced Japanese attitudes toward man in
nature. At the same time, however, the fact that
the public generally respected his desires and
could sympathize with him reflects the degree to
which primeval notions of man in nature, beyond the
ken of many non-Japanese, remain present in the
Japanese mind.

It is important to differentiate between outer
and inner manifestations of Japanese society.
Materially Japan has been undeniably transformed.
But how much has Japan's economic growth transformed
the culture which spawned it? A culture and the
economy it hosts are not independent entities. They
are integrally related to each other. It is because
of this relationship that economic growth is so
greatly influenced by culturally derived attitudes.
The two-way street character of this relationship
is less commonly recognized.

Japanese attitudes toward growth and modernization have a complex history. Integral to that
history is Bellah's conception of the protestant
ethic at work in Japan.[7] The man-nature values
which are embodied in the folk-Shintō related
essentials of Japanese culture were not compatible
with the destructive activities which accompany
modernization and industrialization.

The compartmentalization of values which
developed to accomodate this dichotomy is a crucial
characteristic of modern Japan. It has permitted
the addition of new values without excluding the old
values. The key to this complex of values was well
described by Bellah:

The processes both of economic rationalization
and of political rationalization require a
considerable degree of freedom from traditionalism before they can begin to have an effect
in leading to the development of industrial
society. <u>Virtually the only way this freedom
can be attained is through the re-definition
of the sacred</u>, so that values and motivation

favorable to the rationalizing processes will
be legitimized and traditionalistic restrictions
overcome. [8]   (emphasis added)

The danger present in re-defining the sacred is that,
if carried to an extreme, it can undermine the basis
of the whole society. The pertinent question now is
whether the sacredness which lies within Japan's
inner essence has been defiled sufficiently to
threaten its societal structure?

This question will never be fully answered in
the affirmative unless Japanese society collapses
under the weight of conflicting pressures. A much
more likely prospect is that Japan will remain
threatened by this social quicksand indefinitely.
A negative answer, implying a return to sacred
values whose idealized forms probably never were the
norm, seems an impossibility. The remaining unstable
middle ground implies that Japanese society will
forever remain in transition; never again to be
traditional and never becoming fully modern. In
short, the Japanese have defiled the sacred and have
modernized to a degree. The price they pay now and
will continue to pay in the future is the tensions
evident in Japan between traditional and modern ways.

The Japanese have relied on a policy of
separating economics and politics -- seikei bunri.
This was most evident in the positions Japan held
vis-a-vis the two Chinas. This, as events have
demonstrated, was an artificial and fragilely
contrived position. Despite the pronouncements of
the United States constitution, the normative roles
of politics and religion are closely linked. In turn,
religion and aesthetic-environmental values are also

28

very closely linked. The latter link is as strong in
Japanese culture as it is anywhere. This linkage
between religious, aesthetic-environmental, and
political values is at the core of the Japanese
defilement of the sacred. To defile one portion of
a whole is to threaten the unity of the whole. This
is what the Japanese have done in their quest for
modernization.

As was noted above, the core of traditional
Japanese values is rurally based. Japan's rural and
hamlet life style has been correctly compared to
the American frontier as the base line for their
respective cultures.[9] The analogy is also instructive in that each has undergone a steady decline in
viability and in the process has been the subject
of retrospective idealization. The importance of
Japan's rural heritage in the make-up of contemporary Japanese values is what substantiates those who
argue, along with Bellah, that in Japan "the polity
takes precedence over the economy."[10] The terms
"polity" and "economy" here must be seen in a broad
sociological sense and not in their narrow vernacu-
lar usage.

It is one of the paradoxes of Japan that,
despite the importance of rural-traditional values,
most Japanese today favor the introduction of newer
more modern ways of life.[11] On the other hand, the
Japanese of today remain intellectually and emotionally tied to their rural origins. Anesaki Masaharu,
describing Japan of the 1930s, wrote:

> When one lives in Tokyo and observes the
> changes, both physical and moral, that have
> taken place, one feels that old Japan has gone;

but when a city like Kyoto, or some rural
district, is visited, the changes seem rather
superficial. [12]

For the student of Japan with even minimal knowledge
of traditional Japan, this statement seems doubly
true of contemporary Japan. Many visitors to Japan
today ramble about the islands only to declare upon
visiting some remote hamlet that finally they have
found the "real" Japan. To the extent that the
Japanese continue to return to their rural origins
to replenish their spirits from these regions' deeply
sunk wellsprings, such travellers have a valid point.
However, a far more salient matter is that the
reality of contemporary Japan is to be found in that
portion of Japan which visitors quickly pass through
in their quest for the "real" Japan.

Despite the continued prevalence of rural
values, Japan is an increasingly urban nation. This
trend is evidenced by the shift in population from
rural areas to urban centers. The population of
rural areas (defined as fifty thousand or less)
which was 54.5% of Japan's total population in 1955
is expected to decline to under 20% by 1980.[13]
Japan is quite likely to become the world's first
major urban state. A still unanswered question is:
what effect will mounting urbanism have on Japan's
rurally based value system?

This is a crucial question because the answer
to it will influence the delicate balance between a
growth oriented society and that society's inherent
limits to redefining the sacred. Japanese attachment
to rurally based values in a technologically sophisticated society has permitted the Japanese to

30

compartmentalize their values into areas so that
their aesthetic sensitivities do not interrupt the
continued economic activity of that society. However,
increased urbanism and the transfer of value roots
to urban bases is likely to lessen their ability to
maintain separate and vicariously harmless value
systems.

This transfer has two related effects. Firstly,
the rurally based values are diminished. This
constitutes a further attack on the sacred qualities
intrinsic in Japanese traditional culture. Secondly,
the urban based values which may be expected to
replace rurally based values will probably be some
form of the technocrat's ethic. Such an ethic may
well constitute a death blow to the sacred qualities
upon which traditional Japanese culture rested. In
short, as the group demands of Japanese society --
which increasingly have been equated with continued
economic growth and prosperity -- come into growing
conflict with Japan's rurally based aesthetic
notions of harmonious man-nature relationships in
an age of mass urbanism, the result is anything but
the resolution of internal ambivalences or the
fostering of greater integrity. In fact, internal
tensions are heightened by the value dilemma which
is thereby posed.

SOCIAL PRESSURES FOR CHANGE

Until very recently the Japanese were content
with the ways in which their society was developing.
A nation-wide poll in 1970 indicated that three
quarters of the Japanese people believed they were
living better than they had five years previously.
The same poll found the same percentage to be

31

confident that the future would bring them continued improvement.[14] The Japanese long have had an active concern with __kokumin seikatsu__ (people's livelihood). From the depths of postwar depravation the Japanese have witnessed a great improvement in their living standards. One of Japan's leading economists forecast that Japan's per capita income will equal that of the United States in the 1980s.[15] Such a prediction would once have raised unanimous huzzas from the ranks of the supporters of the national economic "team." However, a growing minority of Japanese now have reservations about such growth and what it means for them and their country.

The Japanese are beginning to doubt the efficacy of equating GNP with living standards and general happiness. Such doubts are by no means universal, but in a society previously so single minded in pursuit of economic growth they are very significant. In part such doubts stem from hard data such as the slower rate of growth in wages paid to labor -- an annual average increase of nine percent during the 1960s -- than the rate of growth in per capita GNP which was over eleven percent annually for the same time span.[16] However, nine percent is not bad and the Japanese did not complain too loudly on that account.

The area which does gall the Japanese is the matter of what they can do with their new-found wealth. The Japanese aesthetic paradigm of a frugal and rustic life style has been overwhelmed with the gadgetry of technological sophistication. Japan is sometimes referred to as an unacquisitive society. This is accurate with regard to the idealized forms

of traditional Japan. There is also some truth to
this appellation as it pertains to Japanese savings
practices within their economic system. However, in
more commonplace contemporary terms, Japan is
becoming the epitome of an acquisitive society. The
Japanese are being glutted with a surfeit of material
possessions. Yet, despite these possessions and
despite the rising GNP "scores", the Japanese --
by and large -- do not see enough improvement in the
quality of their life. As an American economist
specializing in Japan correctly observed, "thus far,
economic growth is making conditions worse, not
better."[17]

Signs of discontent have been growing among the
Japanese. Of greatest significance in economic terms
are the changes evident in the renowned Japanese
work ethic. These changes are most evident among
today's youthful workers -- those who will constitute
the bulk of labor in not too many years. Polls taken
by the Prime Minister's office consistantly indicate
that Japanese workers, particularly the young, care
less about their work and more about their leisure
activities than did their predecessors. Prior to
recession induced fears for job security in the
1970s, Japanese workers demonstrated a significant
shift away from concern over personal security and
toward personal interests and, to a lesser extent,
personal profit.[18] Japan's industrial leaders
recognize this as a problem for their interests.
It is a threat to docile growth at any price.

A principal result of the clash in Japan
between idealized yet supportive rurally based
values and the devastation wrought by gross

industrialization has been the reevaluation of past smugness. The Japanese have had and still retain a certain sense of cultural superiority. This sense has been particularly acute in the realm of aesthetic appreciation of natural beauty. Because of this reputation, partially self-inflated for tourism purposes, the Japanese have become renowned for their sensitivity to nature. Their normal mode has been to look down upon less gifted peoples. It has, therefore, been unsettling for the Japanese to discover that their aesthetic veneer has been tarnished and pitted by the effluent of industrial excesses. The Japanese have complacently assumed that "different" was inherently "better." They had not asked themselves the question asked by Moncrief:

> If non-Judeo-Christian culture has the same levels of economic productivity, urbanization, and higher average household income, is there evidence to indicate that these cultures would not exploit or disregard nature as our own culture does? [19]

Their assumptions were unwarranted as the Japanese discover day by day.

Japan's idealized ways were keyed to the acceptance and glorification of a paucity of material wealth. The rigors and austerity of the past were linked to material poverty. In this regard, one is reminded of Jean Mayer's comment on China:

> It might be bad in China with 700 million poor people, but 700 million very rich Chinese would wreck China in no time. [20]

Even with the saving grace of relatively free trade which -- perhaps temporarily -- relieves the

Malthusian pressures an autarkic Japan would confront, the Japanese are enroute to proving Mayer's point as it might apply to Japan. One hundred million plus increasingly rich Japanese are indeed harming Japan's natural endowment.

The Japanese were, at first, slow to recognize and accept what they were doing to their habitat. Some Japanese still refuse. However, in a world grown leary of ecological and economic catastrophes at some ill-defined point in the future, Japan is increasingly recognized as a test case -- a miner's canary of the advanced world breathing the first poisonous gases seeping out of the Malthusian abyss. What makes Japan such a test case is the physically narrow confines within which the Japanese have managed to squeeze so much industry. Cramped space, plus an operational work ethic which sanctions the violation of the sacred, has yielded pollution of a magnitude sufficient to transform the renowned beauties of Japan's Inland Sea into what one Japanese termed a "vast cesspool."[21]

Several years ago it would have been virtually inconceivable for a Japanese to describe their beloved Inland Sea as a cesspool. That it is no longer unthinkable is a measure of the changing perceptions of the Japanese. Pollution, or in the more comprehensive Japanese term -- kōgai, has become a vital issue in Japan as elsewhere. Delineation of the technical details of Japan's kōgai is not the function of this study.[22] Rather, it is to assess attitudes related to kōgai as they may influence Japan's ecopolitical[23] situation. Not too many years ago it would have been difficult to gauge Japanese attitudes toward kōgai. Despite the evidence swirling around them, the Japanese ignored the swill as the price of progress and contented themselves by reciting their litany of man in nature rhetoric. Now, however, the Japanese have turned about face and are engrossed in problems of the environment.

JAPANESE CONSERVATION

The Japanese have perforce, if belatedly, recognized the ecological havoc their economic activities have wreaked on their physical environment. In a manner reminiscent of Japan's nineteenth century conversions to then foreign processes, many Japanese have switched positions from docile polluters to environmental minutemen. This would seem to be an instance of tenkō, the Japanese cultural phenomenon of making a sudden conversion from ones position or belief to another -- often one quite the opposite of the former stance.[24] The range of emergent attitudes is broad indeed. On the one hand, it reached the extreme of some of Japan's youth romanticizing and idealizing the solitary existence led by ex-sergeant Yokoi in an environment free of all forms of kōgai.[25] On the other hand, the Japanese have produced excellent analyses of what their environmental problems are and what they need to do about them.[26]

Foremost in the Japanese wave of new environmental concern was former Prime Minister Tanaka Kakuei's best-selling book entitled Nihon Rettō Kaizō Ron (A Plan for Remodeling the Japanese Archipelago).[27] In essence this plan called for continued economic growth but growth which would be

36

carefully guided and redistributed more evenly
throughout the Japanese islands. Such growth would
incorporate more attention to social overhead. In
fiscal 1973 the Japanese government adopted a five-
year plan designed to create a "Dynamic Welfare
Society," cutting environmental disruptions by one
half. Central to its environmental programs, the
government adopted the "Polluter Pay Principle"
(PPP) in which firms must pay to correct pollution
related problems which they cause. In addition the
government planned to increase spending on anti-
pollution projects under the five-year plan. All of
this was expected to yield a society which, while
reducing kōgai, would continue to grow economically.

The plans of the Tanaka government were
welcomed by Japan's _Keidanren_ (Federation of
Economic Organizations) as a means to "help the
healthy growth of underpopulated areas."[28]
Approval by Japan's economic establishment of an
environmental action plan is an indication of its
potential efficacy. There were numerous critics of
the plan.[29] In general criticism focused on the
contradictions manifest in proposals to contain
kōgai by fostering greater growth and on the
policies which, in effect, permit a license to
pollute. The latter was particularly pertinent to
the "PPP" system. The direct conflict between
governmental goals and changing popular values
posed the greatest threat to the now dormant
Tanaka plan.

Despite the Tanaka administration's grandiose
ideas for controlling pollution via more growth, the
people via their elected representatives were more

pragmatic about controlling kōgai. The legislature
created a very thorough law entitled the "Basic Law
for Environmental Pollution Control" which clarified
environmental responsibilities for the public and
private sectors and set overall pollution standards.
The legislature also established a "Central Environmental Disruption Countermeasures Headquarters" in
1970 to coordinate nation-wide efforts. This was the
result of the 1969 "White Paper on Environmental
Hazards" which outlined areas of critical importance
for the 1970s. Capping these was the creation in
1971 of the Kankyōcho (Environment Agency) to over-
see all the government's conservation and pollution
fighting activities. The Environment Agency works
closely with other interested branches of the
government. For example, the Ministry of Agriculture
and Forestry initiated a "pollution information
bank" to be used cooperatively by the public and
private sectors to secure data on pollution problems.
Acting in conjunction, the various agencies of the
Japanese bureaucracy produced an extremely comprehensive yet concise statement on Japan's environmental problems and the measures the government was
taking to alleviate them for presentation to the
1972 Stockholm Conference on the environment.[30]

Japan's revised official attitudes toward
environmental issues are indeed heartening. Hard
evidence of these changes can be seen in several
areas. Japan's judiciary, reflecting both public
and official attitudes, has asserted itself in a
series of cases involving kōgai-related social
disruptions. The courts have been severely critical
of advocates of growth at any environmental price.

38

In response to such judicial attitudes Japan's industrial leaders have, albeit reluctantly, decided to increase their efforts in the related areas of conservation and pollution prevention. The government too greatly increased its efforts in this area, notably in research conducted by the Environment Agency's Institute for Environmental Pollution Research. Such activities are noteworthy, but more significant was the government's view set forth in the Economic Planning Agency's September 1973 "White Paper" which suggested that a better life can indeed be had without continued harmful growth. Its 1975 White Paper, calling for slower growth rates, also aided the fight against pollution, but it was more responsive to world economic conditions than to the domestic environment.[31] Nevertheless, this trend is of the greatest importance among a people who were once wholeheartedly committed to growth, growth, and more growth.

Growth as an end in itself has become decreasingly desirable among the Japanese people. They have now expressed a willingness to pay the price for the excesses of Japan's past successes. This willingness is reflected in the growth of environmental action and consumer groups. Such groups are not yet as well developed in Japan as they are elsewhere, but they have made a start and can not be ignored any longer. One of the difficulties with such groups and their motivation is that they do not yet seem to fully comprehend precisely what the costs of Japan's past ecological excesses may be. To correct this situation the Japanese government has undertaken limited educational campaigns to spread knowledge of the extent of Japan's plight.

A greater difficulty related to environmental attitudes and the costs of alleviating pressures is related to a characteristic of Japanese society. The Japanese have in the past succumbed to a succession of fads; each in turn swelling and then subsiding into obscurity. The dangers of faddish interest in "ecology" and "environment" are world-wide dangers. The Japanese are not alone in confronting the cry-wolf syndrome, but because of Japan's experiences with notoriously quixotic fads we have ample reason to question the long term commitment of the Japanese. Whether they will continue to be as obdurate in the future as problems mount remains a serious question.

Central to Japan's future problems are the ecopolitical relationships which the Japanese have yet to fully comprehend.[32] The Japanese have admitted that the good life can be had without environmentally destructive economic growth. This is admirable, but it is a long way from recognizing that such a life can only be had without excessive growth. An environmental ethic which posits the desirability of a relatively homeostatic world economy is glaringly absent from the otherwise excellent Japanese statements on the environment and economics.[33] The Japanese have yet to candidly confront an ecopolitical future of political man struggling for survival in a world of resource scarcities.

PROSPECTS FOR CHANGE

As the Japanese look to the future, they will have to rationalize their attitudes toward natural systems with the emergent realities of a changing world. Attitudes toward natural systems are among

the most complex and subjective aspects of culture.
This is to be expected since the object of interest
is itself infinitely complex. In traditional and
modern Japanese culture nature has been approached
on two levels. However, a gap exists between these
levels. On one level, the aesthetic, the Japanese
have been astute and sympathetic observers of
asymmetry in nature. However, as Anesaki pointed
out, Japanese aesthetic senses have generally
neglected the "many rhythmic motions and regular
processes in the world."[34] On the other level, the
pragmatically scientific, the Japanese have been
very proficient analysts of the inner workings of
the physical environment. Japanese scientists are
renowned world-wide. However, Japanese science suf-
fers from an affliction unfortunately too common
among scientists -- a tendency to view science as
all powerful. Although this predilection is a
world-wide phenomenon, it is particularly acute in
areas -- such as Asia -- which are relatively
recent converts to the scientific method of inquiry.
In between the poles of the aesthete and the
scientific technocrat is the area wherein Japan's
best approach to the ecological perspective may lie.
Natural systems certainly can be understood
scientifically. But it is doubtful that science can
aid humanity in appreciating natural systems.
Appreciation and the cultural attitudes required
are more subjective. What is needed is an ecologi-
cally, and hence scientifically, sound appreciation
of the asymmetrical as well as the symmetrical elements in natural systems. Such well rounded
appreciation is, as Anesaki correctly observed long
ago, frequently weak in Japanese culture.

To date the Japanese have managed to live with this gap between their aesthetic and scientific appreciation of natural systems. They achieved new economic and cultural heights by, respectively, their physical abuse of and abstract love for nature. This seeming paradox enabled the Japanese to prosper. To understand this phenomenon it is necessary to understand the compartmentalization of values which prevails in Japanese society. To favor one stance it is not necessary to disavow another stance. Both may be appreciated in their own sphere. Japanese appreciation of nature has been compartmentalized into segments of their daily routine. Since their notions of "nature" today are quite idealized and abstract, segmentation is not difficult to achieve. Actions in one realm do not necessarily conflict with other activities. While engaged in economic activities their destruction of natural systems is deemed divorced from their aesthetic appreciation of the same systems.

As long as outside sources of materials can permit the Japanese the freedom to avoid the total destruction of their remaining natural areas, this dualism will permit the Japanese to prosper and maintain a certain degree of internal consistency within their segmented ideals. Such compartmental-ization may even be offered as an example to other peoples seeking to maintain a sense of balance with nature in their hectic lives. However, this false duality is essentially illusory and can not be carried on indefinitely. As the ecopolitical situation approaches Malthusian dimensions the pressures to exploit domestically will inexorably

encroach upon the remaining natural enclaves thus
wiping out the illusion that separation can be maintained. Encroachment abroad will have a similar --
if less dramatic -- effect on the Japanese psyche.
It will be inexorable unless the Japanese reorder
their goals and ambitions. With goals in accord with
the ecological paradigm the dilemmas of the future
may be confronted and managed. The price may be high
in terms of attainable aspirations, but it can be
done if the desire is present.

Unfortunately, the Japanese -- as of this
writing -- have given scant indication of recognizing the necessity for such changes. The Japanese,
along with many other peoples, persist in an adher-
ence to science that verges on faith. Unfortunately,
belief in science as a virtual panacea is a common
affliction. The Japanese view of science in their
future was well represented at their exhibits at
Expo '70 in Ōsaka. The Japanese government, in an
exposition of the place of nature and science in
Japan's future, stated:

> The standard of science and technology today
> is regarded as the barometer of the national
> power of a country. Now that her science and
> technology have taken long strides, Japan is
> ranked among the world's most advanced countries
> ..... There will be no bounds to the future
> development of Japanese science and technology,
> which promise the realization of our dreams and
> a fuller living for us.[35]

On the same occasion Mitsubishi Corporation took
immense pride in depicting their role in the ongoing
creation of an artificial environment within which

man would enjoy a better and more harmonious life.[36]
Such reliance on science and advocacy of the creation
of highly vulnerable artificial systems is a formula
contrary to the best of environmental ethics. The
Japanese still have time to correct the error of
their ways. Unfortunately, they do not yet seem to
be prepared to face the central issue of their
future.

The renowned Japanese love of nature still
exists, but it has been diluted by modernization
and its excesses. Japan's representative at the
United Nations' Stockholm Conference in 1972
affirmed Japan's reasons for supporting the conference and its activities as "to eradicate the traditional conquest-minded approach to nature and
instead emphasize a more harmonious relationship
between man and nature."[37] At first glance one
might think the representative had erroneously
attributed such an approach to Japan's tradition
out of ignorance of Japan's true traditions. This
may, in fact, have been the case. However, it seems
more likely that the position of the Japanese government at that time reflected the reality of Japan's
modern "tradition"" -- a tradition which embodies
the conquest-over-nature legacies Judeo-Christian
cultures imparted to the sciences and technologies
absorbed by the Japanese. Contemporary Japan's
man in nature concepts therefore constitute an
amalgam of imperfectly meshed traditions. The modern
Japanese poet, Kitagawa Fuyuhiko, reflected this
blend of concerns

The sun shines in mildly from tall windows,
A humming rises from the steelworks.

44

I got out of bed
And poked with a stick the muck in the ditch;
The turbid water slowly began to move.
A little lizard had yielded himself to the
current.
In the fields
I push open black earth.
The wheat sprouts greenly grow.
-- You can trust the earth.[38]

Whether the Japanese can continue to rely on the
earth in the future is the crucial question to which
we shall now turn.

NOTES

1. Muraoka, Tsunetsugu. Studies in Shinto Thought
(Tokyo, 1964), pp. 29-46.
2. Tsunoda, et. al., Sources of Japanese Tradition
(New York, 1964), Vol. I, pp. 460 and 480-488.
3. Ibid., Vol. II, p. 75.
4. Sansom, George B., The Western World and Japan,
a Study in the Interaction of European and Asiatic
Cultures (New York, 1950), p. 381.
5. Akutagawa, Ryūnosuke. Kappa (Tokyo, 1949), p. 104.
6. Asahi Shimbun Correspondents (compilers), 28 Years
in the Guam Jungle (Tokyo, 1972), pp. 10-11. Yokoi
also stated "I feel like Urashima Tarō". (p. 56)
Urashima is a character in a Japanese fairy tale who
returned home after years spent in an undersea
castle and is analogous to Rip Van Winkle.
7. Bellah, Robert N., Tokugawa Religion; the Values
of Pre-industrial Japan (Glencoe, 1957), p. 5.
8. Ibid., p. 8. See also: James A. Dator, "The
Protestant Ethic in Japan" in George K. Yamamoto

and Ishida Tsuyoshi (eds.), Modern Japanese Society (Berkeley, 1971), pp. 201-209.

9. Burks, Ardath W., The Government of Japan (New York, 1964), p. 53.

10. Bellah, op. cit., p. 5. It is in this sense that the expression "economic animal" is erroneous.

11. In the early 1970s a survey of the Japanese found them favoring newer ways:

Introduce new ways and things	43.3%
Preserve traditional ways and things	25.7
Cannot say indiscriminately	26.1
Unknown	5.0

Japan Institute of International Affairs, White Papers of Japan (Tokyo, 1972), p. 383.

12. Anesaki, Masaharu. Art, Life, and Nature in Japan (Westport, 1971), pp. v-vi.

13. See: James W. Morley, "Growth for What? The issue of the seventies" in Gerald L. Curtis (ed.), Japanese-American Relations in the 1970s (Washington, 1970), p. 67; and Okita Saburō, "Japan and the world economy through the 1970s: a projection" in Japan Report, Special Supplement, 7/16/72, p. 2.

14. Japan Institute of International Affairs, op. cit., pp. 383-385.

15. Okita, op. cit., p. 1.

16. Morley, op. cit., p. 52.

17. Hunsberger, Warren S., Japan, New Industrial Giant (New York, 1972), p. 33.

18. Japan Report, 1/16/72, p. 3; and 7/16/72, pp. 6-7. See also the poll entitled "Survey of Youth Attitudes" (Wakamono Ishiki Chōsa) cited in Okita, op. cit., p. 13.

19. Moncrief, Lewis W., "The cultural basis of our environmental crisis" in Ian G. Barbour (ed.),

<u>Western Man and Environmental Ethics</u> (Reading, 1973),
p. 40.

20. Mayer, Jean and T. George Harris, "Affluence:
the fifth horseman of the apocalypse" in <u>Psychology
Today</u>, January 1970, p. 50.

21. Kunimoto, Yoshirō, "Deserted mountain villages
of western Japan" in <u>Japan Quarterly</u>, January-March
1973, p. 95.

22. While as recently as 1969 more than half the
people polled in Japan were able to respond that
they were free of troubles regarding pollution
(Japan Institute of International Affairs, op. cit.,
p. 394), in the early 1970s a spate of book appeared
in Japan regarding environmental pollution which
indicated an increase in public concern. See for
example: Gotō Kunio, <u>Bunmei, Gijutsu, Ningen</u>
(Culture, Technology, Man) (Kyoto, 1972); Kaji Kōji,
<u>Kogai Gyōsei no Sōtenken</u> (Total Review of Pollution
Administration) (Tokyo, 1971); Kankyō Hōrei Kenkyu-
kai (Environmental Law Research Society), <u>Kōgai
Gairon</u>(Outline of Pollution) (Tokyo, 1972); Katō
Tadoru, <u>Kōgai no Miraizō</u> (The Future of Pollution)
(Tokyo, 1970); Matsumoto Shōetsu, <u>Kōgai to Kihonteki
Jinken</u> (Pollution and Fundamental Human Rights)
(Tokyo, 1972); Taketani Mitsuo, <u>Kōgai Anzensei
Jinken</u> (Safeguarding Human Right (from) Pollution)
(Tokyo, 1972); Ui Jun, <u>Kōgai Retto, 70 Nendai</u>
(Pollution Archipelago, 1970s) (Tokyo, 1972). For
a brief objective statement on Japan's environmental
problems and the initial measures taken to correct
them, see: Allen V. Kneese, et. al. (eds.),
<u>Managing the Environment; International Economic
Cooperation for Pollution Control</u> (New York, 1971),
pp. 185-198 and 339-342. For an up to date overview

of Japanese pollution see: <u>Quality of the Environ-</u>
<u>ment in Japan 1976</u> and subsequent edition published
by the Japan Environment Agency (Tokyo, 1976) as
well as the monthly publication <u>Japan Environment</u>
<u>Summary</u> by the same agency.

23. The term "ecopolitics" -- as used by the writer
-- designates the ecological or environmental study
of politics with emphasis on the effects of environmental constraints (particularly resource scarcity)
on political action, hence eco-politics. Just as
ecology is the holistic study of nature and cultural
geography, with its roots in nature and man's place
therein, is the holistic study of man on earth,
ecopolitics (a stepchild of geopolitics) synthesizes
these holistic views and brings them to bear on
political man and the earth which is his home.

24. Other examples of this are the switch to right-
wing militarism by some pre-war leftists and the
sudden transformation of left-wing students who
"sell out" and become staunch company men after
their graduation.

25. Asahi Shimbun Correspondents, op. cit., p. 114.

26. In addition to the works cited in note 22, see
especially: Hoshino Yoshirō, <u>Hankōgai no Ronri</u>
(Logic of Anti-pollution) (Tokyo, 1972).

27. Tanaka Kakuei, <u>Nihon Rettō Kaizōron</u> (Remodeling
the Japanese Archipelago) (Tokyo, 1971). The book
reportedly was ghostwritten: TIME, 1/29/73, p. 26.
Hoshino Yoshirō states that the book's sales were
poor until Tanaka became prime minister, in
"Remodeling the archipelago" in <u>Japan Quarterly</u>,
January-March 1973, p. 44.

28. <u>Environmental Pollution and Japanese Industry</u>
(Tokyo, 1973, first edition), p. 4.

29. For an excellent survey of opposition party criticism of Tanaka's plan, see: Nihon Rettō Kaizō-ron Hihan (Criticism of Remodeling the Japanese Archipelago) (Tokyo, 1972).

30. Information Bulletin 1970 (Tokyo, 1971), pp. 183-187 and 116-120; Japan Institute of International Affairs, op. cit., p. 432; and Japan Report, 11/16/73, p. 8. For the Stockholm report, see: Problems of the Human Environment in Japan (Tokyo, 1971).

31. For a discussion of the courts and pollution in Japan, see: "Pollution case law" in Japan Quarterly, July-September 1973, pp. 251-254. The Economic Planning Agency's white paper is summarized in Japan Report, 10/16/73, p. 8. The 1975 white paper is covered in "A new road to a stable economy" in Focus Japan, November 1975, pp. 13-15; and in U.S.-Japan Trade Council Report Number 32, June 1976. The attitude of Japanese industry toward pollution control is well covered in Keidanren Papers, Number 5, Environmental Pollution and Japanese Industry (Tokyo, 1975, revised edition). Details of court cases and pollution issues are described in Kōgai Benran (Handbook on Environmental Pollution) (Tokyo, 1972). The problems of mediating between industry and environmentalists in Japan are described in "Real environmental countermeasures" in Economist, July 1976.

32. See note number 23.

33. Most Japanese would reject any notion of the desirability of a declining economy as suggested by Georgescu-Roegen, see p. 6.

34. Anesaki, op. cit., pp. 18-19.

35. Nihonkan, Nihon to Nihonjin (Japanese Pavilion,

Japan and the Japanese) (Osaka, undated, ca. 1970),
pp. 19-20.

36. <u>Mitsubishi Miraikan, Nihon no Shizen to Nihonjin
no Yume</u> (The Mitsubishi Future Hall, Nature in Japan
and the Dreams of the Japanese) (Osaka(?), undated,
ca. 1970).

37. <u>Problems of the Human Environment in Japan</u>, op.
cit., p. 17.

38. Quoted in Donald Keene (ed.), <u>Modern Japanese
Literature</u> (New York, 1956), p. 379.

Chapter 4

JAPAN, A NEO-MALTHUSIAN STATE

MALTHUSIANISM AND JAPAN

Two hundred years ago Thomas Malthus postulated
the well known doomsday scenario of mounting population confronted with material scarcity, yielding a
catastrophic collision with the supportive capacity
of our planet. Malthus' theory has frequently been
met with derisive ridicule. He is charged with
ignorance of economic adjustment mechanisms which
anti-Malthusians assure us will always compensate
for the pressures Malthus cited in support of his
theory. The underlying contention of this study is
that, despite the ability of adjustment mechanisms
to temporarily ameliorate Malthusian perils and
postpone the day of reckoning, Malthus' theory has
never been effectively disproven.[1]

A corollary contention -- and the focus of this
study -- is that Japan is very probably the foremost
candidate in the industrialized world to become a
Malthusian state. Given the relatively greater
capacity of non-industrialized states than industrialized states to more readily absorb the impact of
Malthusian setbacks by accomodation,[2] as the most
vulnerable in a highly vulnerable category Japan is

potentially the world's leading Malthusian state.

Malthusianism is a spectre which long has lurked in the shadows of Japan. The Malthusian perspective is not presently a popular view of Japan. In addition to the dangers of being considered an "environmental determinist," the past experience of those choosing to apply Malthusian analysis to Japan has been full of pitfalls. Instead, in this chapter we shall analyse Japan's position utilizing an environmental possibilist perspective with Malthusian overtones. We thereby trust we can avoid the pitfalls which have entrapped those who came before.

In contrast to currently prevalent assumptions that Japan is at long last free of the Malthusian dilemma, the pre-war period's assumptions about Japan were almost universally Malthusian. Japan's needs for resources and geopolitical lebensraum (living space) for her confined but growing population were seen as motivation for her expansionist policies. These circumstances were seen in the same light within Japan and abroad, although the respective reactions to a territorially expansive Japan were understandably different. That these assumptions were commonly held and were acted upon does not make them any more true. As Moulton and Marlio correctly observed -- in a prescient but little known work, The Control of Germany and Japan -- Japan at that time was not in truly Malthusian straits. They correctly based their view on the seldom recognized circumstances of Japan's original economic growth in the Meiji period. Rather than seeking autarky, Japan's initial modernization was founded on the ready abandonment of economic isolationism in favor of extensive international free trade based upon natural specialization and the application of modern science and technology to the emergent processes of production both in industry and agriculture.[3] Societal adaptation thereby overcame existing natural handicaps.

The difficulty with Malthusian predictions in the 1930s was that they approached a self-fulfilling prophecy. The Japanese were considered expansive and grasping. Consequently they had to be restrained. Attempts at restraint and concurrent economic embargoes led the Japanese to cherish the notion of self-sufficient autarky. Such autarky could only be achieved by fulfilling the prophesies of Japan's detractors -- that is, by territorial expansion. Thus a vicious circle was created which brought about Japan's participation in the Second World War.

The allegedly "Malthusian" circumstances of the pre-war and wartime eras were decidedly man-made phenomena. The same can be said of the postwar era, although in different and lessening respects. In the immediate postwar period Japan was confronted with conditions which some Malthusian analysts saw as a paradigm of Malthusianism. They were wrong. A gross example of such Malthusian views was that of the respected demographer, Warren Thompson, who stated in the early 1950s:

> The outlook for restoring the living conditions of Japan's people to pre-war levels in the near future is quite discouraging, to say nothing of the outlook for improvement beyond that level.[4]

The weakness in the allegedly Malthusian assessments of Japan in the past was their failure to anticipate

the ameliorating effects of social institutions. Man
created the difficulties Japan was in and man was
able to extricate Japan.

Contemporary Japan seems to belie most early
postwar analysis. To the degree that this is true,
it is due to the social institutions of international commerce. As Moulton and Marlio correctly
observed, Japan's loss of both colonies and con-
trolled access to foreign resources would only have
been debilitating if one assumed the Japanese
posited goals of near-autarky. Barring such goals,
they saw no obstacles to Japan's economic revival
in a free-trading world.[5] Their prescience is
amply evinced by Japan's postwar economic recovery
and rapid growth to levels undreamt of in the
pre-war era.

Japan's postwar economic success and the fact
that previous Malthusian scares were artificially
induced does not mean that the spectre of Malthusianism has waned. Neither the Japanese nor any
other people have yet had to confront a world in
which other states were constrained from free and
open trade, not by fears arising from political
artifice, but by fears arising from limits imposed
by their recognition of their own dependency upon
finite resources. Such a world would be significantly different from that which has previously
placed Japan in pseudo-Malthusian peril. In this
regard the neo-Malthusian view of Harrison Brown,
circa 1954, is instructive:

> Today Japan is confined once again to her home
> islands, and the pressure of her population is
> now far greater than it was prior to World War

Two. She must import a substantial portion of
her food and raw materials, yet she is cut off
from many of her former sources of supply. In
the long run her situation is unstable in the
extreme, and it is highly likely that serious
trouble lies ahead. The Japanese now express
the desire to live in peace with other nations,
but as time goes on and the pressures become
still more intense, it is likely that they will
attempt again to extend their area to the point
where they can attain some measure of self-
sufficiency.[6]

Reading this in the last quarter of the century it
appears outdated and too tied to concepts of Japan's
needs more appropriate to the 1930s. But is it
really? Though Brown was undoubtedly influenced in
this analysis by the prevailing postwar pessimism
about Japan's immediate economic prospects, the
"long run" he utilizes as an analytical framework
in his writings is not the economist's long run of
a single generation. Instead it is the ecologist's
longer frame of reference. This is a crucial
difference. If we assume Malthusian pressures of
high population and increasingly scarce resources
will mount in the coming decades throughout the
world and reach a climax -- probably between the
turn of the century and the middle of the next
century[7] -- what will Japan's alternatives be? In
this portion of this study we shall address the
importance of scarcity to Japan. The concluding
chapter will address the issue of Japan's alternatives.

POPULATION

Environmental pollution (kōgai) is a serious issue in Japan, but it is merely the tip of the Malthusian iceberg. Forming that "iceberg" are the relationships between Japan's population and its access to both agricultural and industrial resources. To better evaluate our contention that Japan is a highly vulnerable state each factor of the Malthusian balance as it effects Japan will be assessed in turn.

It was said of pre-war Japan that "Japanese foreign policy will be determined by her population problem."[8] While such a Malthusian pronouncement should have sounded strange then, since Japan was in reality beset by pseudo-Malthusian circumstances (e.g., socially solvable conditions), it did not. However, it certainly would not ring true to the ears of many today. The works of Irene Taeuber and others, stressing Japan's dramatic seizure of control of a once burgeoning population and its promise of continued stability at a level of one hundred twenty to thirty millions through the end of the century,[9] have led to the prevalence of assumptions that Japan no longer has a population problem. In the sense that Japan's population has indeed stabilized[10] such assumptions are undoubtedly valid. The Japanese are justly proud of their achievements in the control of population growth and take an active leadership role in Asian population planning sessions. However, as demographers are wont to point out, population numbers do not tell all. Such numbers must be seen in some context.

If one assumes that conditions of resource availability and world trade will remain amenable to Japan's interests, then the role of Japan's stabilized population would not be a significant determinant of the future. However, such assumptions are not made here. In contrast, under assumptions of a finite world, a rapidly increasing global population, and increased competition among the earth's masses for the resources a finite world can produce, the needs of Japan's population -- albeit relatively stabilized -- again becomes a crucial factor. In order to understand just how crucial a factor the needs of Japan's population might be, we must examine Japan's resource base.

AGRICULTURAL RESOURCES

The frugal and industrious character of Japanese agriculture has permitted it to develop apace with and foster the economic growth of modern Japan.[11] This is not meant to imply that Japanese agriculture has been problem-free, for it was plagued by both natural and social problems.[12] Leading the list of Japan's agricultural problems was the simple fact that Japan's arable land, which is only fifteen percent of its total land area, has been unable to support a large population on its own. By means of such techniques as using intensive labor, more double cropping via new seed varieties adapted to Japan's colder areas, and inter-culturing and rotation of crops the Japanese have been able to increase greatly the yields of their principal crops -- notably rice.[13] Japan's reliance on primary rather than secondary crop consumption[14] is itself a cultural adaptation to finite land resources.

In response to past pressures for self-sufficiency in food production Japan's agriculture became
very labor-intensive. It appears now to have reached
a point where further application of human labor
would be both land- and labor-inefficient. As a
result the Japanese have successfully supplemented
their labor-intensive agriculture with small scale
mechanization.[15] This development in Japan has had
an additional facet. Japanese agriculture reached a
peak of land-use efficiency, but by surpassing that
peak the returns diminished in terms of labor-
efficiency. Highly land-efficient agriculture is
inherently labor-inefficient. As a result Japan's
agriculture yielded a great deal of underemployment.
This, in turn, contributed to the migratory appeal
of urban areas. However, as farm labor left the
land, it had to be compensated for especially during
planting and harvesting seasons. Hence the enhanced
role of machines in Japanese agriculture. Mechanization is reflected in Japan's rural social structure
in which approximately one-third are full-time
farmers, while the other two-thirds are part-time
farmers.[16] As in so many other Japanese instances,
Japanese agriculture presents a paradox. Japanese
agriculture is undoubtedly among the most labor-
intensive in the world, but, in terms of investment
in machinery per unit of land, Japanese agriculture
may also be the most mechanized in the world.

Japanese agriculture, despite its advances, has
reached a stalemate with the pressures of a large
population on a small amount of land. Japan's
agricultural sector does a remarkable job of meeting
Japan's food needs. Nevertheless, as the following

chart indicates, Japan's ability to feed itself has declined over the years:

Table 4.1

SELF-SUFFICIENCY RATES OF AGRICULTURAL FOOD PRODUCTS

(Unit: %)

Category	Fiscal Year							
	'60	'65	'66	'67	'68	'69	'70	'71
Overall Rate	90	81	80	84	83	80	76	72
Grains	83	61	59	63	62	56	48	42
Rice	102	95	101	115	118	117	106	92
Wheat	39	28	21	20	20	14	9	8
Barley,Rye	107	73	65	59	60	48	34	29
Beans	44	25	19	20	17	14	12	11
Soybeans	28	11	9	8	7	5	4	4
Vegetables	100	100	100	100	100	100	99	99
Fruits	100	90	89	89	88	85	84	81
Eggs	101	100	100	99	98	98	97	98
Milk and Products	89	86	80	82	88	91	89	88
Meat (no whale)	91	89	89	84	82	82	88	83
Sugar	18	30	27	28	26	24	23	20
Overall Rate (including seafood)	93	85	84	87	87	84	81	77

Note 17

Moreover, Japan faces consistent projected short-falls which -- as the following chart suggests -- will leave it dependent on and vulnerable to foreign food suppliers:

Table 4.2

PROJECTED SELF-SUFFICIENCY RATE OF

PRINCIPAL AGRICULTURAL PRODUCTS

(Unit: %)

Category	FY 1972 Actual Rate	FY 1985 Estimated	Growth
Overall Rate	73	75	2
Rice	100	100	-
Vegetables	99	100	1
Fruit	81	84	3
Eggs	98	100	2
Meat (no whale)	81	86	5
Milk, Products	86	94	8
Sugar	20	28	8
Wheat	5	9	4
Barley, Rye	18	36	18
Soybeans, total	4	9	5
Soybeans (for human consumption)	20	60	40

Note 18

The Japanese long ago recognized that their agricultural posture was akin to that of the British. Neither can sustain their desires for food domestically. Both conceive of themselves as industrial states supplementing their indigenous capacity by bartering for food from their positions of economic natural advantage. In Japan's case these circumstances have been magnified by social and biological changes. While the Japanese people may not grow much larger in numbers, they have been growing in body size and weight.[19] These physically larger Japanese require greater amounts of food to meet their minimum needs. Moreover, Japanese palates have undergone a transformation from a desire for a spare fish and rice diet to a more exotic and plentiful variety of foodstuffs, many of which are comparatively wasteful of land resources. The oddity here is that while Japanese rice production has increased, the domestic demand for rice lessened as the Japanese acquired a taste for imported foods. Despite the superficial appearance of adequate or over-production of the traditional Japanese rice diet, Japan's new food desires have made Japan more dependent on foreign sources. The "wasteful" land resources that the Japanese utilize to meet their acquired tastes are generally located abroad. It is doubtful whether the Japanese (or the English) could ever make the transition back to an agriculturally autarkic economy. If a reverse course were ever compelled by inadequate foreign supplies, the costs in human suffering would be stupendous.[20]

Recognizing their dependency and poor prospects for relieving themselves with their own land resources, the Japanese are making a major effort to supplement their food production via both traditional fisheries and aqua-culture.[21] Harvesting the natural produce of the seas is vital to Japan. Seafood and laver (edible seaweed) constitute important sources of protein and minerals in the Japanese diet. However, the limits of this natural harvest are already becoming apparent as national rivals stake out their legal claims to offshore and deep sea ocean areas. Japan's technological innovations in the science of aqua-culture are important and promise to provide some room for growth in domestic food production. However, here too, the scope for improvement appears to be constrained by competition. Such restrictions on all aspects of potential food production from the seas make it unlikely that Japan can find surcease from food pressures by turning away from the land.

The agricultural wealth of the relatively underpopulated lands is not a bottomless pit. Bearing in mind the need to view the carrying capacity of the earth as "flexible limits,"[22] rather than firm boundaries, world agricultural resources are distinctly limited. These resources are also threatened by climatic fluctuations which -- in addition to the comparatively manageable hazards of periodic droughts and floods -- threaten to reduce arable land by thrusting the earth into another neo-boreal period or "little ice age."[23] Agricultural production is also threatened by the gradual spread of the world's deserts.[24]

Nations whose economic natural advantage is in the industrial sector may in the future find themselves hard pressed to sell their inedible manufactures for increasingly scarce foodstuffs. The Japanese are squarely in this category. Despite their confident rhetoric and hopes that technological innovations may relieve them, the Japanese can scarcely hope to achieve more than the prevention of a further increase in Japan's dependence on food imports.[25] Hence, Japanese warnings to food producing peoples to be less protectionist or the Japanese will turn to alternative markets has the distinctly hollow ring of a person whistling in the dark. Such a strategy will work only as long as food is freely traded. As population pressures mount world-wide the stage will be set for a crisis of

agricultural production. Initially market forces
will enable the Japanese to cope with the emerging
crisis by paying higher prices for imported food.
In the very long run, however, global pressures on
food production promise to bring about harsh competition for food which will hobble free trade and
sharply restrict Japan's options.

INDUSTRIAL RAW MATERIALS

Reference to Japan's economic natural advantage
in the industrial sector of the global economy must
be held up to further scrutiny. Japan is a great
industrial nation. However, unlike many other
industrial giants, Japan did not originally achieve
this status on the basis of a wealth of indigenous
natural resources. Rather, Japan's industrial might
was achieved despite its paucity of natural
resources. It was based essentially on Japan's
wealth of human resources. Japan's industry was
built upon readily available foreign sources of raw
materials and Japan's hard working, skilled, and --
then -- comparatively poorly paid labor. Japan's
economic cycle of imports and finished exports
yielded a system which R.B. Hall correctly termed
the "world workshop."[26]

Japan's poor domestic natural resource base is
one of the best known attributes of the Japanese
economy. Japan is deficient in almost every raw
material ordinarily deemed essential for the creation and operation of a successful industrial
economy.[27] Japan approached this deficiency in two
ways. Firstly, the Japanese have, via the "Natural
Resources Development Law" of 1950 -- later

63

subsumed within the Economic Planning Agency
(Keizai Kikaku Chō) -- attempted to identify and
exploit all of Japan's usable resources.[28] These
activities have been carried out most extensively
in Japan's more pristine natural areas, notably
Hokkaidō, and, while enhancing production, have been
quite destructive of Japan's remaining natural
environment. These economically necessary but
environmentally harmful activities have added
further force to the plaints of Japan's environmentalists.

Secondly, and far more important, the Japanese
have forsaken their immediately pre-war and wartime
goals of enforced assured access to sources of raw
materials in favor of a return to the assurances
of free-trading nations that they will supply Japan
commercially with its required raw materials. This
second facet of Japan's approach to its natural
resource deficiency is the keystone of Japan's
postwar economic resurgence. To date this policy
has been very successful. As Herman Kahn correctly
noted:

> Fortunately for the Japanese their scarcity of
> indigenous material resources does not now seem
> to make much difference. They are tapping the
> entire world for raw materials, and because of
> the scale on which they do so and the technolo-
> gy they use, in some respects they enjoy
> cheaper raw materials than any other nation
> in the world.[29]

Moreover, as Kahn and Hout sought to emphasize, the
percentage of foreign trade within Japan's economy
has declined to less than ten percent of Japan's

64

GNP -- a rate lower than both pre-war Japan and
many contemporary European states -- and the percentage of imported raw materials within the total GNP
has steadily declined.[30] Such views are in accord
with the standard economic view of the declining
role of raw materials within technologically
sophisticated economies. This trend is not denied
here -- for the present. However, the future is
another matter.

The trends Kahn and Hout indicated are somewhat
misleading in the current context for two reasons.
First, assuming Japan's GNP continues to grow --
albeit at a slower pace -- and despite a possible
decline in the percentage of GNP which is dependent
upon resource imports, in absolute terms the amounts
of resource imports may well mount apace with a
growing economy. Since GNP is measured in monetary
terms, in an inflationary world the percentage
alloted for natural resources by Japan may well grow
in both real terms and, at a faster rate, in monetary terms. Second, regardless of its rate of
growth, Japan clearly will remain dependent upon
foreign sources of raw materials. Japan's high rates
of dependence (indicated on the following table) are
both undeniable and eminently important in a world
sensitive to growing scarcities.

Table 4.3

DEPENDENCE ON IMPORTED NATURAL RESOURCES

Category	FY 1970	FY 1974
Copper	76%	90%
Lead	55	80
Zinc	55	64
Aluminum	100	100

(continued)

Nickel	100	100
Iron Ore	88	99
Coking Coal	79	72
Petroleum	99.7	99.7
Natural Gas	35	74
Uranium	100	100

Note 31

Further complicating Japan's resource dilemma are Japan's periodic efforts to increase exports to help pay for more costly imported resources. Not only do these export drives tend to foster protectionist sentiment in Japan's foreign markets, they also tend to increase the overall vulnerability of all sectors of the Japanese economy to the frailties of resource dependency by linking the fortunes of more sectors to a growing need to pay more for imported resources.

Japan's economic success story, based on a dearth of indigenous raw materials, is analogous to the helicopter. At first glance neither should work, but both do. Fortunately, the helicopter's ability to remain aloft is based on immutable laws of aerodynamics. The Japanese economy's continued well being, however, rests upon the forbearance of other peoples. Should that forbearance be dissipated by the stresses of Malthusian catastrophe looming on the horizon, the Japanese economy is barely removed from the proverbial "accident looking for a place to happen."

What does the future hold for the Japanese economy and resources? The energy "crisis" of 1973-1974 is something of an indicator of the future, but for the wrong reasons. The energy crisis' causes were political -- not physical -- but its symptoms

66

were virtually the same as those some future endemic resource shortage would create. The Arab reduction of oil supplies to the Japanese, among others, clearly demonstrated Japan's critical dependence on foreign supplies of a necessary commodity. A prominent Japanese economist predicted at that time that Japan "will tend to dominate world trade in natural resources" to the extent of fifty percent of the total world trade in iron ore and twenty percent of the total world trade in petroleum by 1980.[32] Another way of saying this is that in a world increasingly subject to and aware of resource scarcities, Japan is enroute to becoming even more dependent and hence vulnerable than it already is. The more Japan's economy expands in a world conscious of commodity-based political power the more intense its vulnerability will become. Until the Arab oil producers pressed the issue, not many non-Japanese were ready or willing to assess the impact of this issue on Japan's future.[33]

The Japanese have not been hesitant to address the narrowly economic problems posed by specific resource inadequacies[34] -- such as in the case of energy. Japan is grossly dependent on foreign sources of energy. While Japan's economic establishment lays a disproportionate portion of the blame for Japan's energy vulnerability on the government's acquiescence to demands for nuclear restraint by Japan's environmental activists,[35] the reality is simply that Japan's domestic sources of energy resources are relatively static and the economy is not. The following data on Japan's projected energy requirements reflect a growing economy.

Table 4.4

PROJECTED ENERGY NEEDS

(Unit: 10 Trillion Kcal)

Category	FY 1973	FY 1980 (estimate)	FY 1985 (estimate)
Hydraulic	18	22	26
Geothermal	0.06	0.6	3.6
Domestic Petroleum and Natural Gas	3.5	6.0	13
Domestic Coal	14	13	13
Nuclear	24	23	68
Imported LNG	32	27	56
Imported Coal	45	71	80
Imported Oil	296	365	440
TOTAL	383	530	710

Note 36

Although alternative energy sources make this
one of the more promising areas of the resource
dilemma in the very long run,[37] in terms of short
run (twenty to thirty years) dependency on foreign
sources, the Japanese now are going from bad to
worse. The Japanese answer to the facts of dependency prior to the Yom Kippur War of October 1973
was formally presented in Japan's first energy
"white paper" issued by the Ministry of International Trade and Industry (MITI) in September of 1973.
This position paper recognized that Japan's needs
for energy were growing more rapidly than those of
the world at large -- a twelve percent annual
increase vs. five percent, respectively. However,
it sought to find the answer to Japan's dependency
in terms of domestic conservation and international
commercial cooperation.[38] Unfortunately for the

Japanese, Arab tactics in the wake of the war clearly demonstrated that dependent nations cannot suffice solely by conserving that which they do not possess. As a result the Japanese became very conscious of their need for the cooperation of interdependent trade partners.

Japan's plight during this period was symptomatic of a Malthusian dilemma but differed in its origins. Just as the problem had a purely political cause, its solution -- from Japan's perspective -- was politically manageable. The Japanese reaction when threatened by the OPEC oil boycott was simply to shift its political orientation toward the Arab position on Middle East issues -- a shift which was not too difficult to achieve in view of Japan's past slighting of Israel.[39] Japan's maleable foreign policy shifts appeased its Middle Eastern suppliers and the life-blood was again turned on for Japanese industry.

The Japanese public has been made only too well aware of their country's dependency on foreign sources of energy and raw materials.[40] Although the Japanese have been ready to address these issues for some time -- if they are narrowly defined -- they have been very hesitant to look at them in ecopolitical terms.[41] The "engineering perspective" is strong among the Japanese. They have -- by and large -- yet to question the assumption that some sort of solution can be found. The alternatives implicit in denying this assumption have been too ominous for them to willingly consider them.

In their quest for a solution to their raw materials problems the Japanese massively increased their overseas investment which they carefully couched in the rhetoric of global interdependence and cooperation with resource-rich but less developed countries. Of the following amounts nearly half have been devoted to resource extractive projects, with the resources destined for Japan's hungry industrial maw.

Table 4.5

JAPANESE OVERSEAS INVESTMENT

Fiscal Year	Cumulative Value*	Percentage Increase Over Previous Year
1951-1964	790	--
1965	949	20%
1966	1,176	24
1967	1,451	23
1968	2,008	38
1969	2,673	33
1970	3,577	34
1971	4,435	24
1972	6,773	53
1973	10,270	52
1974	12,666	23
1975	15,943	26

(Unit: U.S.$ Million)*   Note 42

During the summer of 1973 the Japanese, expecting shortages, began to act as international hoarders by buying whatever current excesses or future production they might secure.[43] They met with mixed success at best. Economic recession and adjustment to higher prices subsequently lessened the short term pressures on Japan. However, as they look to a future of revived resource scarcities, the Japanese are increasingly wary of unspoken coalitions of

70

environmental activists and economic nationalists in
the resource-rich nations whose programs would
retard Japan's access to its foreign sources of
supply.[44]

MALTHUSIAN PROSPECTS

Japan, the economic giant with embarassingly
visible feet of clay, faces potentially dire
straits. Economic adjustment mechanisms, resource
substitutions, and new technologies for the development and utilization of new or underutilized resources will undoubtedly enable Japan to at least
temporarily cope with neo-Malthusian pressures with
varied success. However, in the very long run, the
Law of Entropy seems certain to gradually have a
negative impact on Japan's ability to cope successfully with a changing milieu.

Moreover, the impact Japan's efforts to cope
with this emerging long term dilemma will have on
Japan's societal base and its international ties
remains in doubt. If Japan's efforts to cope with
neo-Malthusian forces in the political guise of
commodity power enervate its domestic social
stability and the rationale behind its dominant
growth ethic and also disrupt the cooperative efforts
of interdependent advanced economies to develop
joint means to manage a dilemma they share, Japan
may well be forced to confront a stark neo-Malthusian future with its options severely curtailed. This
prospect is the subject of the concluding portion
of this study.

NOTES
1. Moreover, the argument is unlikely to be settled

71

within the time span of anyone now living. Among the
recent Malthusian studies of interest are: Energy:
Global Prospects 1985-2000 by the Workshop on Alternative Energy Strategies at the Massachusetts Institute of Technology, 1977; and a reported secret
document describing the social upheaval which energy
shortages could create -- cited in the Jack Anderson
column, Washington Post, April 5, 1977, p. B15.
The Club of Rome which sponsored The Limits to Growth
reversed itself somewhat in 1976, TIME April 26,
1976, p. 56, but retained its ultimate pessimism by
stating that disasters will be inevitable if international cooperation fails.
The use of the term "Malthusian" in this study is
broadly generic, though -- as noted in the introduction -- this study draws upon the theoretical
work of Professor Georgescu-Roegen as well as
Malthusian theorists. For a more complete explora-
tion of the author's views of Malthusian theory, see
"Ecopolitics: Malthus revisited" in Susquehanna
University Studies, June 1977, pp. 153-167.
2. Due to their inherent ecological stability
attributable to a more autarkic order of existence
and a simpler sponge-like regenerative task in the
wake of a disaster.

3. Moulton, Harold G. and Louis Marlio, The Control
of Germany and Japan (Washington, 1944), pp. 76-81.

4. Thompson, Warren S., Population and Progress in
the Far East (Chicago, 1959), p. 117.

5. Moulton and Marlio, op. cit., pp. 76-81.

6. Brown, Harrison, The Challenge of Man's Future
(New York, 1954), p. 235.

7. Serious difficulties stemming from physical shortages seem likely to emerge within that time span, leading in time to the sort of crises described in this study. Though global crises will probably mount slowly and gradually, as noted below, Japan's problems seem likely to crystallize in the earliest phase of a developing process.

8. Crocker, Walter R., _The Japanese Population Problem, Coming Crisis_ (London, 1931), p. 214.

9. Taeuber, Irene B., _The Population of Japan_ (Princeton, 1958); and "Japan's population: miracle, model, or case study" in _Foreign Affairs_, 1962, pp. 595-604. See also: John T. Takeshita, "Population control in Japan" in George K. Yamamoto and Ishida Tsuyoshi (eds.), _Modern Japanese Society_ (Berkeley, 1971).

10. The Institute of Population Problems of the Ministry of Health and Welfare offers the following data on the number of children per couple in surveys taken from 1940 to 1972:

1st Survey		(1940):	3.39	Children
2nd	"	(1952):	3.30	"
3rd	"	(1957):	2.79	"
4th	"	(1962):	2.31	"
5th	"	(1967):	2.20	"
6th	"	(1972):	1.92	"

Cited in _Japan Report_, 10/16/73, p. 5.

11. Two excellent studies of Japan's agricultural and economic growth are: T. Ogura, _Agricultural Development in Modern Japan_ (Tokyo, 1963); and Okawa Kazushi, et. al., _Agriculture and Economic Growth: Japan's Experience_ (Princeton/Tokyo, 1970).

12. Recognizing that "natural" in the East Asian cultural landscape sometimes means man-induced, e.g. floods and landslides. Foremost among the problems Japan faced was soil erosion, see: Graham V. Jacks and Robert O. Whyte, The Rape of the Earth: A World Survey of Soil Erosion (London, 1939), pp. 85-92. Most of the natural and social problems were alleviated by better management arising out of the postwar efforts in land reform, see: Ronald P. Dore, Land Reform in Japan (London, 1959); and Laurence I. Hewes, Jr., Japan -- Land and Man, An Account of the Japanese Land Reform Program - 1945-51 (Ames, 1955).

13. Ogura, op. cit., pp. 14 and 26.

14. For a discussion of this reliance, see: Glenn T. Trewartha, Japan, A Geography (Madison, 1965), p. 221. Such an adaption yields an emphasis on human consumption of foods that are of a lower trophic level. That is, they are lower on the food chain. Rather than eating the animal protein derived from animal consumption of lower foods, men in such circumstances rely on direct consumption and bypass the intermediate stages. The principal benefit of this adaption is that more men can survive per unit area of land if they are primary consumers than if they are secondary consumers.

15. Trewartha, op. cit., pp. 198 and 209-210. See also James P. Grant, "Development: The end of trickle down?" in Foreign Policy, Fall 1973, pp. 49-50.

16. Ishida Ryūjirō (Isida Ryuziro), Geography of Japan (Tokyo, 1961), pp. 63-65.

17. Focus Japan, November 1974, p. 20.

18. Ibid., April 1975, p. 5.

19. This point is made by Richard Storry, "Japanese attitudes to the West" in Raghaven Iyer (ed.), The Glass Curtain Between Asia and Europe (London, 1965), p. 132.

20. For an assessment of rice production in Japan, see Danno Nobuo, "The changing face of agriculture" in Japan Quarterly, July-September 1972, pp. 296-298. The limited improvements in Japanese agricultural production must be modified by the fact that although Japan's population increases about one percent per year, its demand for foodstuffs has increased about seven percent per year as its people's wealth increases.

21. For a contemporary look at Japanese aqua-culture see the Washington Post, 6/1/77, p. A18.

22. See Chapter 1, pp. 2-4.

23. This thesis received a great deal of publicity as a result of a leaked Central Intelligence Agency study (later published) which surveyed climatological research and was cautiously pessimistic; Washington Post, 5/2/76, p. A2. An equally pessimistic thesis contends that pollution will produce a "hot house" effect within the earth's atmosphere, leading to rising temperatures, melting polar ice, and the flooding of low lying coastal areas.

24. This threat is serious enough to warrant holding the Kenya Conference on "desertification" in August 1977 under United Nations auspices.

25. For an account of Japan's hopes for food produc-

tion, see U.S.-Japan Trade Council Report No. 18, *Japan's Domestic Food Policy*, April 13, 1976.

26. Hall, Robert B. Jr., *Japan: Industrial Power of Asia* (Princeton, 1963), p. 43. Faith in the power of Japan's human resources to pull that country through difficult times is quite resilient. For example, see former Prime Minister Miki's comments in a speech opening the 77th Diet: "Poorly endowed as she is in natural resources, the greatest blessing that Japan has received from heaven is her people. It is the people of Japan who, harboring limitless potential, are Japan's most precious treasure." *F.B.I.S.*, 1/26/76, Asia, p. C5. (Emphasis added).

27. Trewartha, op. cit., pp. 66-97, provides a list of scarce resources. Edward A. Ackerman, *Japan's Natural Resources and Their Relation to Japan's Economic Future* (Chicago, 1953) provides useful, if somewhat outdated, data. Takai Fuyuji, et. al., *Geology of Japan* (Berkeley, 1963), also provide a thorough, if narrowly focused, assessment of Japan's available domestic resources.

28. Burks, Ardath W., *The Government of Japan* (New York, 1964), pp. 177-178.

29. Kahn, Herman, *The Emerging Japanese Superstate* (Englewood Cliffs, 1970), p. 96.

30. *Ibid.*, p. 111; and Thomas Hout, *Japan's Trade Policy and U.S. Trade Performance* (New York, 1973), p. 20.

31. Ministry of International Trade and Industry, *White Paper on International Trade* (English edition by Japan Trade Center), (Houston, 1976); and

White Paper on "Prospect of Natural Resources
Problems in Japan" (JETRO Economic Report No. 1)
(Tokyo, 1972).

32. Okita Saburō, "Japan and the world economy
through the 1970s: a projection" in Japan Report,
Special Supplement, 7/16/72, pp. 3-8.

33. One who was and was criticized for being an
overly cautious "wet blanket" was economist Henry
Rosovsky who questioned Japan's ability to sustain
its past rates of growth in the future, in "Japan's
economic future" in Challenge, July-August 1973,
p. 17.

34. For examples of book length Japanese attempts
to assess Japan's resource situation, see: Aono
Tadao, Kigyō to Kankyō (Business and the Environ-
ment) (Tokyo, 1971); Itagaki Yōichi, Nihon no Shigen
Mondai (The Resource Problems of Japan) (Tokyo,
1972); and Keizai Shingikai Shigen Kenkyu Iinkai
(Economic Review Society, Resource Study Committee),
Kokusaika Jidai no Shigen Mondai (Resource Problems
of an Internationalized Age) (Tokyo, 1970). An
interesting panel discussion on Japan's position
regarding global mineral resources appeared in
Keidanren Geppo, June 1974.
On energy, see: Japan Institute of International
Affairs, The Oil Crisis - Its Impact on Japan and
Asia (Tokyo, 1974); "Running out of energy" in
Focus Japan, May 1977, pp. 8-9; and "Energy: the
long-range supply-demand situation" in the Ministry
of Foreign Affairs' Information Bulletin, 8/15/77,
pp. 1-2.

35. Environmental Pollution and Japanese Industry
(Tokyo, 1973, first edition), p. 10.

36. Economic Planning Agency, Economic Plan for the Second Half of the 1970s (Tokyo, 1976), p. 155.

37. Several alternatives are discussed in Japan. On nuclear power, see: Kishida Junnosuke, "Atomic Energy Development at a New Stage" in Asahi Journal January 17, 1975. On solar energy, see the special issue on "The Sunshine Project", Focus Japan, January 1976. One author looked to Japan's future need for energy and offered a unique proposal -- develop Arabic studies in Japan. See: Katakura Kunio, "The future of energy and resource problems" in Gaiko Jiho, June 1975.

38. Japan Report, 11/1/73, p. 8; and 12/16/73, pp. 1-3.

39. For assessments of Japan's previous treatment of Israel, see: Washington Star-News, 11/22/73, p. A-12; and TIME, 7/19/71, p. 18.

40. U.S.I.A. sponsored polls indicated in 1974 that eighty five percent of university educated Japanese and seventy eight percent of the Japanese general public knew that obtaining oil was a serious problem for Japan. Ninety eight percent of the university educated and eighty six percent of the general public knew that Japan's dependence on other countries for its raw materials was from "consider-able" to "very great." See: United States Information Agency, Office of Research Study No. R-16-74, Japanese Attitudes on Important Economic Issues, December 31, 1974.

41. A step in that direction was taken by publishing a collection of articles in Japan Echo under the collective title, "The vulnerable power", Vol. IV,

No. 1, 1977, pp. 17-79. A more Malthusian view was expressed by a leading Japanese economist, Ichimura Shinichi, at a 1975 symposium entitled "Seeking a New Japan in a Changing World Economy." However, the majority of other economists attending the symposium disagreed with Professor Ichimura's pessimism. See: Asahi Evening News, 7/1/75, p. 4.

42. Japan's Overseas Private Investment -- Growth and Change (Washington, 1973), pp. 1-5; and Ministry of Finance Statistics ending FY 1975 (March 31, 1976). These data were calculated on an approval basis, e.g., actual disbursement may not have reached the stated levels in the year cited.

43. For contemporary coverage of Japan's activities, see: TIME, 8/20/73, pp. 70-73.

44. See, for example: Taira Koji, "Power and trade in U.S.-Japanese relations" in Asian Survey, November 1972, p. 989, who warns: "Ecologists in the U.S. today may be inadvertently playing into the hands of economic nationalists by their attempts to block the supply of resources to Japan in the name of environmental protection."

Chapter 5

INTERNATIONALISM, ECONOMIC VULNERABILITY,
AND POLICY OPTIONS

JAPAN'S REACTION TO A CHANGING WORLD

Former Prime Minister Yoshida Shigeru once
presciently called upon his countrymen to develop
"far-reaching vision and the ability to assume our
rightful role in the ever widening arena of international relations."[1] Yoshida was well ahead of his
time for in the intervening years the Japanese
continued to drag their feet and maintain foreign
policies euphemistically termed "dual diplomacy."
The Japanese became notable for their international
reticence and timidity, characterized by evasive
maneuvers and the avoidance of hard decisions on
vital issues. The result of such policies was
international benignity which permitted Japan's
economic resurgence. This was, of course, in Japan's
best short-run interests. However, it created
difficulties for the political long-run. In the
process of acquiring a benign reputation the Japanese sacrificed much of their former inner élan.

It was not until Japan's burgeoning economy
reached huge proportions that the Japanese again
thought of themselves in global political terms.
By the late 1960s Japan's "new realists" sought to

80

take advantage of both the Sino-Soviet split and the emergent detente between the United States and the Soviet Union to recover some of Japan's lost international political stature. As in the pre-Commodore Perry period, Japan was on its way toward change when events intervened to provide the extra nudge to speed up the process.

1970 saw Ōhira Masayoshi[2] urge the Japanese to stop thinking of themselves as perennial "international outsiders" and start to think of themselves as "insiders" by involving themselves more thoroughly in international affairs. The transition to a post-postwar period was underway. The watershed was reached during the years 1971-1972. During that interval the Japanese regained full sovereignty over the Ryūkyū Islands and experienced the series of so-called "shocks" centered on U.S.-Japan economic and diplomatic relations. The reversion of Okinawa had been forecast by former Prime Minister Satō Eisaku in 1965 as the event which would signify the end of the postwar period for Japan.[3] In reality, however, it was the "shocks" which forced the Japanese to recognize the watershed from a postwar to a post-postwar era. The United States, as a result of domestic and South-East Asian considerations, had decided to reduce its military role on mainland Asia and step back from its confrontation with the Chinese. Japan, although not the direct object of these policies, was caught up in the American retrenchment.

A principal result of these rapid changes in East Asian international relations was the abrupt and forced expansion of Japan's place in the East

81

Asian sub-system. Although the Japanese had been
tentatively planning some renewed activity, the
speed with which their role was enlarged startled
and upset them. The sudden introduction of a
relatively larger sub-systemic role for Japan was
also unsettling to the overall international system
in which the triangular relationship between the
United States, the Soviet Union, and China clearly
had been dominant.

The external imposition by changed circumstances of a larger role was not widely welcomed by the
Japanese. In reaction they pulled in their feelers
and regrouped to reassess where they stood and
where they wanted to go. At this writing they
remain cautiously pensive. In time some Japanese
policy initiatives appear inevitable, but a sweeping
announcement should not be expected. As a rule the
Japanese are not interested in grand designs. With
some notable individual exceptions, as a people they
do not now seek a unique role for Japan. Utilizing
their as yet limited political capital in the
pursuit of tangible commercial gains, the Japanese
generally accept the existing framework of international relations as a reality to which they will
accomodate themselves.

Japan's past use of "dual diplomacy" is
analogous to the mechanics of a _yajirobei_ -- a
Japanese toy which, balancing on a vulnerable
vantage point, bends to outside forces of gravity
and wind, but manages to right itself. Both the
yajirobei and the Japanese adopt a reactive rather
than a manipulative style. However, an underlying
contention of this study, that future resource

scarcities will revive and reinforce rivalries among nation states, threatens to severely shake the vantage point of free trade which Japan -- a national _yajirobei_ -- uses as a fulcrum.

The rivalries probably will be felt most strongly and immediately by those states most heavily involved in international trade and especially by those among the latter which are technologically sophisticated and materially vulnerable. This is a prescription for Japan. By 1980 and beyond the Japanese economy, though smaller than those of the United States and the Soviet Union, will nevertheless have a great impact on the international system. Although Japan's economic slump in the early 1970s may make Japan's impact by the 1980s somewhat less pervasive than it might otherwise have been, a substantial impact is still anticipated by most observers of international economic relations. However, what will the nature of the impact of Japan be if one makes dire long-term Malthusian assumptions? States such as the United States or the Soviet Union can be expected to absorb initial shocks and, if the proper adjustments are made to each system, to come to an accomodation eventually. Both supplier states and states with smaller economies will probably withdraw behind protective barriers and attempt to make the best accomodations they can to the new circumstances which they will confront. It is the economically advanced, technologically sophisticated, and materially vulnerable states led by the countries of Western Europe and especially by Japan which seem likely to suffer first and most. Can Japan successfully adjust to

the new economic forces at work in international
relations? This is the question to be examined in
this concluding section.

ECONOMIC VULNERABILITY AND SHORT RUN POLICY

Yoshida Shigeru once described his nation's
postwar economic growth as a "dream" to those who
had experienced the immediate postwar collapse.[4]
As a result of Japanese economic vulnerabilities
that dream is in danger of becoming a nightmare in
the foreseeable future.

Japanese officials recognize that the circumstances which permitted them to adhere to a doctrine
of separating economics from politics (seikei bunri)
in their generally successful postwar economic
diplomacy (e.g., American primacy in Asia, ready
access to Third World resources, etc.) are changing.
Japan's freedom to be an economic actor in a
political play is lessening. Just as world leaders
have come to accept the economic importance of
major political decisions, increasingly the Japanese
recognize the political nature of many key international economic issues. Somewhat more reluctantly
the Japanese have agreed to enter the political
forums in which these issues will be resolved.

In recent years the Japanese have been tempted
by contemporary political circumstances to equate
their economic power with power in a larger political sense. As the power-as-force aspects of political power ebbed in an age of nuclear stalemate, the
role of the economic facets of power have increasingly come to the fore. Thus the Japanese have had
the logic of contemporary political alignments

behind them in their quest for new recognition as a world power.

However, claims to power based on economic prowess are dependent on other factors. These "other factors" may be partially military, but in the prevailing condition of nuclear stalemate this is not necessarily so. This is particularly true of Japan with its legacy of military excesses. To the Japanese, with their economy fragilely dependent on international goodwill and their active memories of defeat in World War Two, the prospect of international military involvement is profoundly disquieting. They have consistently disavowed any large scale military ambitions.

A more important criterion of economic power, in a world in which the raw materials underpinning economic and -- by extension -- military power are becoming recognized as finite and scarce commodities, is a degree of self-determination in resource matters sufficient to free a nation from pricipitate and willful severence by another state. In Japan's case the roots of its power are set in infertile soil and must be force-fed from external sources. Thus Japan's expressed desires to become a world or a regional power based virtually exclusively on its economy is fraught with dangers.

Japan's dependence on foreign suppliers of food and raw materials is its Achilles heel. The decline of the percentage of raw materials within the total Japanese GNP and the initiative of Japan's renowned human "resources" have given many observers of the Japanese economy reason to hope that its vulnerabilities may not prove debilitative. However, it is

both undeniable and eminently important in a world
of mounting scarcities that Japan will remain dependent on foreign sources of raw materials indefinitely. Japan's economy -- and its international political weight -- rests upon the forbearance of other
peoples.

The Japanese are severely disquieted by the
threat posed to them by "commodity power" in the
hands of their suppliers -- singly or in cartel. It
has undermined their longstanding effort to separate
economics from politics. Significantly commodity
power also threatens Japan's political response to
the threat of commodity power. Japan's response,
diversifying its dependence, is now a key aspect of
its international economic policy. By diversifying
trade and investment the Japanese hope both to
diffuse the impact of Japanese economic growth on
the world economy and to reduce the prospect that
Japan may be held hostage by its suppliers. The
former is important to Japan's short-run political
and economic relations. The latter is vital to
Japan's long-run foreign relations. Like a skilled
practitioner of the martial arts, the Japanese hope
to get by with adroit shifts of position and subtle
maneuvers rather than relying on their fragile sheer
strength. However, in the very long-run, the economic strengths of the wielders of commodity power
threaten to restrict Japan's room for political
maneuvering.

While several important suppliers are industrially advanced countries (notably the United States,
the Soviet Union, Australia, Canada, New Zealand,
and South Africa), many others are developing

86

countries. In the near term Japan has little reason
to be concerned about being cut-off by its advanced
suppliers, but the LDCs are another matter. Japan is
under mounting pressure from its Third World
suppliers over North-South issues. In Latin America,
Brazil, Mexico, Peru, Venezuela, and Cuba are important to Japan. Its ties with the oil producers of
the Middle East are vital to the Japanese economy.
In Asia, Japan focuses on South Korea, Indonesia,
the Philippines, Thailand, Malaysia, Australia, and
-- with some uncertainty -- on China and Taiwan.
Although Japan's interests in Black Africa remain
relatively small, they are mounting in Nigeria,
Zaire, and Zambia. As that continent's productive
capacity expands, Japan's interests there may well
expand apace. Japan's diversified interests in a
broad range of countries promise to temporarily
reduce the threat of economic blackmail by single
suppliers, but the shift to relatively greater
emphasis and partial dependence on poorer regions
of the world makes Japan even more susceptible in
the long-run to the combined pressures of a class
of countries attracted to the concept of commodity
power.[5]

Working to eliminate the threat posed by
commodity power and forestall heightened consumer
nation competition, Japan made gradual and tentative
moves toward reasserting the global economic
commonweal in the wake of 1975's Rambouillet
Economic Summit, 1976's Puerto Rico Summit, 1977's
London Summit, and the 1977 Conference on International Economic Cooperation (CIEC) -- of which
Japan was a co-chairman of the Raw Materials Commi-
sion. These moves were supported by Tokyo's

reassessment of the domestic implications of economic growth in an age of resource vulnerability first presented in the Economic Planning Agency's 1975 White Paper. The paper, arguing for a slower pace of economic growth to permit Japan to adjust to the constraints of the times, enumerated the following factors: 1) trends in world business cycles among industrialized countries which make them prone to global inflation and slumps, 2) generally tighter supply-demand situation for food and raw materials, and 3) relatively more concern over environmental conservation -- albeit at some cost in production efficiency. The 1976 and 1977 White Papers reinforced this assessment.[6] Supporting Japan's new found commitment to slower economic growth, the Japanese government's fiscal 1976-1980 five-year economic plan called for Japan to follow "a growth path with limited leeway" for some time. The six percent growth rate called for in the plan is the second lowest of the target rates in past economic plans.[7]

Under the guidelines of self-imposed (but externally necessitated) slower planned economic growth the Japanese hope to successfully contend with emerging international economic pressures. Accompanying a somewhat less dynamic economy, the Japanese continue to present a benign international political facade. Fondly focusing on their dual role as a probably unrealistic North-South "bridge" between the industrialized advanced countries and Third World peoples and a more pragmatic advocate of mutually beneficial global interdependence, the Japanese eschew the risks inherent in tough choices. In this respect, their style has not changed. How-Japan's admittedly hesitant willingness to address

the political implications of international economic
issues is, nevertheless, a significant step forward.
Japan's go-slow foreign and domestic economic
policies may appear timid, but they serve Japan's
national interests well by holding open a range of
future options in an era which seems likely to be
marked by economic flux and political uncertainty.

As long as the short-run choices remain Japanese choices, the Japanese are unlikely to deviate
from their safe middle course. However, Japan's
potential economic vulnerability promises to make it
difficult for the Japanese to retain full control of
their destiny in the future. Japan's economic vulnerability is so acute that most Japanese perceive
their plight as akin to the stance of happo-yabure
in the martial sport of kendo which implies
defenselessness on all sides.

THE POLITICS BEHIND POLICY

The politics behind contemporary Japan's
economic and foreign policies is a rather non-ideo-
logical politics of consensus. The conservative
ruling Liberal Democratic Party (LDP) -- which has
competently guided Japan since World War Two -- is
a brokerage party of competing factions led by
politicians wielding a personalized brand of power
over their followers, cemented by the leaders'
ability to dispense money and influence. In contrast
the opposition parties are more ideological and
generally less successful. The LDP has been very
successful in leading Japan to a postwar resurgence
of which the Japanese people are intensely and
justly proud. As long as the proven policies of the

pragmatic LDP continue to work, there is little prospect that the Japanese will press for fundamental change -- though a coalition of the moderate center no longer appears unthinkable.

In the midst of this apparent tranquility Japan's vociferous left wing parties -- most notably the Japan Communist Party (JCP) -- took the lead in challenging the LDP's lack of progressive environmental and Third World policies. The Communists and the Japan Socialist Party (JSP) initially captured the protest vote in this area. Though the vote totals of the major left wing parties slipped markedly in 1976 and 1977 Diet elections, their reputation as recipients of the environmental protest vote seems to have survived their setbacks intact. However, the LDP is preeminently a pragmatic party. Quick to shift with the tides of change, the LDP is virtually certain to accomodate its economic and political policies to Japan's emerging environmental and economic needs. This transition will be promoted as the LDP comes to recognize the inherent linkage between their economic-environmental stance and the already well understood Japanese need for a secure economic niche in a well meshed global community of nations.

A key aspect of Japan's political process, common to all its parties, is that the consensual policy making process is far more reactive than it is manipulative. Since the emerging issues in international economic relations of importance to Japan are strongly imbued with ideological overtones, the Japanese opposition parties would seem to have a slight edge at the outset. They seem to be ideologi-

cally prepared to react to the challeges the future
poses. In fact, appearances are probably deceiving.
The opposition parties' ideologies are quite dogma-
tic. They do not have the requisite reactive flexi-
bility to shape effective policies.

In vivid contrast, the relatively non-ideologi-
cal LDP (or its structural successor as a brokerage
party -- regardless of its name) is fully capable of
making the political transition which Japan's place
in a changing world will probably require. As a
result, Japan's ruling factions -- reacting to
changing circumstances -- are likely to incorporate
ideological considerations as they shape Japanese
policy somewhat more in the future than they do now.
Since the formula for political success and social
stability in Japan is likely to remain the consensual process, the anticipated greater ideological
polarization will probably remain within ruling
party circles. Assuming the challenges Japan will
face are sufficiently obvious, increased ideological
factionalism should not unduly disrupt the policy
making process in the ruling party. However, it may
lead Japan's policy makers in the future to consider
policy options which today would be considered
beyond the pale by its contemporary conservative
elite.

THE U.S. CONNECTION

The linchpin of Japan's role in the international system is its relationship with the United
States. Evolving from a _deshi_ (devoted student)
status in the occupation period, Japan's relationship with the United States now is approaching a

semblance of reciprocity. Both countries profess shared perspectives on the international situation. We affirm a common commitment to an open world trading system, a stable monetary order, detente with the communist states and world peace, stability in Asia, and diversification and assured access to energy and raw materials sources. In these and many other areas we both contend things have never been better in our bilateral relations. However, while it is true that many values and interests are held in common, important long range differences persist.

These differences go beyond the still present gap between the Orient and the Occident. The latter can be coped with as each other's cultural frame-work is better understood. More important are the significantly different legacies the United States and Japan bring to bear on the much ballyhooed relationship of multilateral interdependence in which we each assert an integral role.

Japan brings its panoply of vulnerabilities, trusting its partners -- large and small -- will foster shared access to the global economic pie. The United States, in contrast, knows it can fall back on its own domestic cushion if cooperation fails. With these different mindsets each country has participated in multilateral forums in recent years to resolve such issues as Japanese capital and trade liberalization, coordination of economic and technical assistance programs, and planning for resource development and assured access to supplies in the LDCs. The significance of many of the impor-tant bilateral issues of late is that virtually all of them have implications extending beyond the

context of U.S.-Japan relations. That relationship
has become inextricably bound to the emerging complex of regional and global institutions which will
underlie the future world order.

As long as their perspectives in these forums
mesh well, the United States and Japan can be
expected to cooperate to their mutual benefit. A
serious question exists, however, as to whether that
harmony would persist in the context of the sort of
mounting Malthusian pressures which this study
presupposes.

The Japanese clearly are eager to reduce their
economic dependence on the United States. Their
progress in this regard already has reduced some of
the psychological strains between the two countries.
However, the Japanese government is somewhat
ambivalent about these trends. They want some
attenuation of the bonds, but not enough to threaten
the bonds' existence. The Arab oil embargo of 1973,
the potential threat of commodity power in the hands
of LDCs gripped by resource nationalism, and strains
in U.S.-Soviet detente underline Japanese vulnerability to Japanese strategic planners.

The United States, in turn, has its own
ambivalence. The United States does not want Japan
to be excessively dependent on the United States,
but neither does it want the Japanese to let loose
of the United States' "apron strings." Japan's
overall potential -- albeit highly vulnerable --
remains a very valuable asset for any country able
to channel it to its own interests. Despite the
costs in expended American defense dollars, occasional Japanese self-centeredness and lack of

compassion for American interests, and some very long term risks that Japan's economic weaknesses eventually may prove to be a liability to the United States, the United States government continues to support Japan steadfastly in bilateral and multilateral arrangements.

JAPANESE OPTIONS IN A CHANGING WORLD

Current Japanese policies may be short-run palliatives. At their worst these policies may have a placebic effect leading the Japanese into a false sense of complacency which would become startlingly apparent if the world economy one day abuts the Malthusian dilemma. As a result of the sense of unease felt by the Japanese as they look to the future, they will probably find it necessary to more rigorously examine the alternative options.

As viewed from a neo-Malthusian perspective, there are four basic options open to the Japanese under two general and opposing assumptions of world order. The general assumptions are a world society marked by increasing levels of competition for a dwindling resource base vs. a cooperative world society sharing access to limited resources on an equitable basis. Operating within the framework encompassed by these two opposing assumptions, the Japanese have four basic alternatives:

Alternative 1: Non-action

Avoidance of the controversial yet quintessential normative issues inherent in the problem has been characteristic of and central to Japan's approach to the two assumptions. Not choosing and permitting inertial momentum to carry societies

94

blithely onward is tantamount to a form of choice.
Non-action is an evasive option and as such has had
great appeal so far to the Japanese who see their
alternatives sharply constricted by their fragile
vulnerabilities and abject reliance on international
goodwill and cooperation. However, the age of non-
action is largely past for the Japanese. They cannot
afford the risk it entails of subjecting Japan's
future to the interests and vagaries of outsiders.

Alternative 2: Territorial Expansionism

Confronted with a jéjà vu scenario of its pre-
war handicaps the Japanese might consider territorial expansionism again as a means to guarantee
control of needed raw materials. They might also opt
for renewed right wing militarism. However, due to
the bitter memories of Japan's defeat, a strong
strain of leftist pacificism in the Japanese body
politic, the dubious abilities of its current armed
forces, and the probable negative reaction to any
Japanese expansionism on the part of Japan's Asian
neighbors and the global community, this activist
option is decidedly the least viable for Japan.

Alternative 3: Negotiated Self-sufficiency

Most of the world's leading nations have
stressed cooperative measures to share access to raw
materials. However, they also prudently maintain
that they would never permit themselves to be held
hostage by foreign powers for a strategic commodity.
The modified self-sufficiency of such cautious
policies admits the possibility of dramatic swings
of the pendulum of world order. Such a position is
a luxury the Japanese cannot afford. Japan does not

have the capability to withdraw within itself for there is little within with which it might sustain itself. That flexible option is effectively closed to Japan.

In its place, if the Japanese government assumes that future resource scarcities will revive and reinforce rivalries among states in their quest for assured access to requisite resources, some degree of negotiated self-sufficiency in resource affairs becomes a desirable goal. The attainable level of self-sufficiency will be determined by Tokyo's assessment of the degree of competition Japan is likely to confront and by foreign reaction to Japan's economic and political negotiating offers.

Any rivalries which may develop will be felt most immediately and strongly by Japan as a state which is heavily involved in international trade, technologically sophisticated, and materially vulnerable. The Japanese are and will indefinitely remain economic hostages to their suppliers -- they must pay the price. As shortages intensify, however, the economic price for negotiated self-sufficiency will become both more difficult to meet and -- to the degree the price is tinged with unwelcome political overtones -- more difficult to accept. This was graphically illustrated in the Japanese reaction to the political pressures exerted by Arab oil purveyors in 1973-1974. In exchange for turning on the oil spigot the Japanese paid a political price in their relations with Israel and, more important, that country's American supporters.

This episode also demonstrated another facet of Japan's dilemma of vulnerability related to negoti-

ated self-sufficiency. Japan faces two types of
resource scarcities: politically induced scarcities
and physical scarcities. The Japanese may successfully seek some degree of limited negotiated self-
sufficiency against the prospect of future politically induced scarcities --e.g., stockpiling oil
against the threat of another Arab oil embargo. Just
as a problem has a political cause, its solution --
from Japan's perspective -- may be politically
manageable. Although it may be economically, politically, and emotionally costly, such "self-sufficiency" is attainable. However, self-sufficiency in a
setting of true physical scarcity -- the long term
Malthusian threat contemplated here -- is an entire-
ly different matter. Neither negotiated limited
self-sufficiency nor maleable political appeasement
will necessarily suffice to extricate Japan -- or
any similarly vulnerable country -- from dire
physical shortages of global proportions. Consequently the present option has severe inherent
constraints.

Alternative 4: Cooperation

The Japanese long had a policy of one sided
free trade. They sought to maximize their exports,
but placed protectionist obstacles before imports
which might harm their economic development. Their
rationale was both protectionist and nationalist in
the sense that they sought to preclude foreign
investments in Japan which might weaken Japan's
control of its own economic destiny. As Japan's
economy blossomed further in the post-postwar years,
these arguments lost their validity in the eyes of
Japan's competitors. Moreover, changes in Japan's

world economic role occured as world-wide concerns over resource scarcities heightened. This led to Japan shedding its cloak of protectionism in favor of a new advocacy of two-way free trade. Japan now realizes that its most vulnerable weakness is not the old fear of direct foreign economic control but its critical needs for commercially reliable sources of industrial raw materials. In the long run this weakness may pose an equally real threat of foreign control of the Japanese economy -- albeit indirect. Realizing the plight which it faces, Japan is rapidly becoming the leading advocate of free-trade among the advanced economies.

This reversal reflects a longer range posture of the Japanese. In recognition of their acute vulnerability they increasingly advocate an option of equitable cooperation among the consumers and suppliers in the global economy. In accord with that stand the Japanese government has frequently and explicitly denounced the shortsighted standpoint of national interests in presenting their case for cooperation. This option posits a world order of nearly utopian dimensions in which neither closed regionalism nor hegemonic selfish interests obstruct the freedom of peaceful and equitable transaction. This world order obviously does not correspond to extant conditions in the international system. Nevertheless, as a goal it is admirably suited to Japan's needs.

The prospects for such a utopian alternative are grossly poor. Although U.S.-Japan cooperation can be safely assumed for some time to come, Japan-European cooperation is less assured. Both Japan

and the states of Western Europe face similar problems and neither fully sympathizes with the other.
Each views the other as culturally remote and
economically competitive. As a result it will be
difficult to create an atmosphere conducive to
generating any real cooperation over access to
resources. It could be argued that the Japanese and
Europeans will eventually come to see themselves as
sharing a common dilemma with consequent common
interests and that such shared perceptions will
foster a united front among these industrially
advanced states. This may occur, but Western
Europe's slightly stronger position regarding
domestic supplies of raw materials plus its closer
historical ties with former colonial areas in the
less developed but resource-rich regions are likely
to produce some reluctance on the part of Western
Europeans to ally themselves economically with a
country -- Japan -- which the Europeans see as
confronting in the future even more dire straits
than their own.

Japan's access to the resources of the communist states of Eurasia is also problematical. Today's
smaller communist states of Eastern Europe and
South-East Asia do not have great potential as
suppliers of raw materials to Japan. They have
limited resources and a growing need for them at
home. China has some potential as a supplier of
resources, but its current policies of non-reliance
on outsiders and its own enormous future needs seem
likely to curtail any prospect that China will
become a major supplier of Japan's resources. The
Soviet Union, on the other hand, has great resource

potentials. However, continuing political strains in Japan-Soviet relations have hobbled the development of economic ties between the two countries. The Soviet Union could conceivably become a major and proximately located source of raw materials for the Japanese in the future. It is even conceivable that a symbiotic economic relationship may develop between Japan and its Soviet neighbors, with Japan receiving resources in exchange for technological and financial assistance. For this to occur, however, the Japanese would necessarily pay a stiff price in terms of compounding their resource dependency by acquiring a new and probably equally onerous political dependency.

Japan's alignment with the third and forth worlds' resource producers may be compelled by economic imperatives, but it will be difficult for third and fourth world peoples to either forget Japan's past expansionism and its causes or to accept Japan as an equal. Such states may legitimately question Japan's magnanimity were the tables turned. Considering the degree to which Japan has scrupulously looked to its economic self interests in the past, the answer is manifest. Despite Japanese rhetoric about a world without borders and the evils of narrow national interests, they advocate international cooperation precisely because it is in their national interest. The Japanese once again have demonstrated the wisdom of the hoary dictum "where you stand depends upon where you sit."

PROSPECTS FOR JAPANESE POLICY

As the Japanese confront the future and consult
these four options (or variations) on a spectrum of
assumptions ranging from a world commons to Darwin-
ian competition, they probably will choose the
lesser evil. Non-action almost certainly will be
rejected because it implies the virtual addication
of their perogatives in determining their future.
Total self-sufficiency also probably will be
rejected for it is unattainable short of implement-
ing a highly irrational expansionist option. The
Japanese are therefore likely to have recourse to a
utopian cooperative option as a means of negotiating
a degree of commercial "self-sufficiency."

Advocacy of utopian propositions may seem
foolish, if the very long run outlook for global
cooperation remains bleak. But what else can Japan
-- or any other vulnerable state -- do? Japan must
seek to rationalize the combined dilemma of gross
economic vulnerability, a pacifist polity, and a
changing domestic context of slower economic growth
increasingly incorporating and complicated by the
ecological paradigm. Alternatives other than a
utopian level of cooperation threaten -- in the very
long run -- to yield catastrophic results. Nevertheless, such results might come in the event a utopian
safeguard failed. Recognizing this bleak prospect,
Japan's policy makers are likely to assume --
probably out of resignation -- that utopian idealism
is pragmatic in Japan's circumstances. In this sense
the Japanese propensity for seemingly fuzzy-thinking
idealism, so often criticized by foreigners in the
past, would seem to be central to their avoidance

of the Malthusian dilemma. For Japan today -- and particularly for tomorrow -- idealism is realism.[8]

In the "short" run (for the next generation or two) Japan's policy makers are likely to follow an intermediate option combining a hope for limited negotiated self-sufficiency based on equitable commerce, stockpiling for "rainy days," and reliance on more truly self-reliant trade partners. Unlike Westerners who seem generically unwilling to resort to mid-range incremental decision making when confronted with major problems, the Japanese do not insist on concrete game plans for their future. As long as scarcities are politically induced and they can maintain the essential duality of economic and aesthetic values in their national polity, the Japanese will retain their outlet in political expediency. However, in time, as scarcities become acutely physical and the resultant pressures on Japanese social values magnify Japanese reactions, the Japanese are likely to confront the tragedy of the commons.[9] As this crisis of secure access to requisite materials approaches, the Japanese are likely to turn first to the utopian alternative of equitable cooperation referred to in the previous paragraph. If this fails or appears likely to fail, the Japanese may well become desperate in the future.

We hypothesize here that the Japanese -- if they are permitted the opportunity by time and rivals -- may well one day resort to a less egalitarian variant of cooperation. Recalling Japanese society's ability to rapidly shift gears to meet new circumstances, Japanese cooperation in a period

of severe crisis need not be cooperation directed by
the present genre of Japanese conservative leaders.
A possibly viable option in dire circumstances,
where its Western allies cannot adequately meet
Japan's resource needs, is the creation of a left-
wing corporate state. Japan might have experienced
such a state in the pre-war period has the semi-
socialist military faction of that time (the kido-ha)
prevailed over the rightists. The lead in the
creation of such a state in the future would probably not be the armed forces -- unless they vastly
increased their stature in the intervening years.
Instead, pragmatic political interests of the
center-left might well take the lead in the creation
of such a state by building upon a long tradition of
corporate paternalism. The advantage of such an
entity is that it would enable Japan to assert
itself as a full-fledged member of resource rich
pan-Asian, Third World, and left-wing states. As
such it could seek to legitimately secure access to
those communities' stocks of available resources in
order to fulfill a role as an industrialized leader
in their midst.[10] Although this type of option
might be narrowly focused and exclusive, it is more
likely to be seen as a supplement to Japan's ties
to a West no longer capable of fully meeting Japan's
needs. In this sense this sort of purely hypothetical option could be of value to the West in the
future by maintaining Western stability as well,
since it would reduce Japan's liability to the West.
The problems of creating such a state and of its
ready acceptance by Asians and others chary of
Japan's motives obviously would be immense. Therefore its likelihood cannot be rated very high.

Nevertheless, if Japan becomes sufficiently desperate, this type of mutant cooperative alternative probably will remain a real option.

Japan's final option will always remain territorial expansion. Japan would have to be at rope's end before attempting it again. However, by that juncture expansionism probably would be too late to suffice. Moreover, in its then weakened condition, Japan could easily be stalemated.

The thrust of this study is that Japan's dilemma of growth, vulnerability, and an ambivalent polity is acute. In the very long run the prognosis is gloomy. Remedies may be found by the Japanese and they may be aided by coordinated policies on the part of Japan's trading partners. But they may not. The dilemma Japan can expect to confront is a global dilemma. Japan is among the nations of the earth least well situated to cope with this emerging complex of crises. It is not impossible that the Japanese -- despite their and their partners' best efforts -- will fail to deal successfully with the dilemma. In that event the international community will have to face a totally new and peculiar problem: what to do with the first nation-state casualty in the battle of industrial states for their continued survival. The problems are not Japan's alone; they are shared by the entire world community.

IMPLICATIONS FOR THE INTERNATIONAL COMMUNITY

If the future of the world indeed proves to be of Malthusian proportions, the international community will face many challenges as succeeding generations attempt to cope with severe shortages by

104

either harsh competition or always tenuous cooperation. An important aspect of this situation will be
the ways in which the relatively self-sufficient
states perceive and deal with those less fortunate
states. Japan's future place in the international
community is likely to be central to this issue of
the future.

The Albatross Hypothesis

The prospect exists that Japan -- today a
vitally important member of the international
community -- may someday in the future be transmuted
by its vulnerability to Malthusian pressures from
the Pheonix of the postwar era into a worrisome
"Albatross" slung around the neck of its allies and
trade partners. The writer hopes this hypothesis is
far-fetched and extreme, but fears it is not. If
Japan, as well as the rest of the global economic
community, play their cards right, the worst may
well be avoided for a long time. But it may not.

On the assumption that a true Malthusian dilemma
is a real possibility in the lifetime of children
now alive, Japan's ongoing efforts to diversify its
sources of supply should be strongly encouraged. We
should also seek to encourage the Japanese to be
pragmatic about idealism as realism in their future.
Although Japan's trade partners should not now
express untoward concern to the Japanese that Japan
may fail to cope with possible neo-Malthusian
economic crises in the future, it would be an error
not to tacitly prepare for that possibility within
our own councils. It is not in the international
community's interest to instigate a self-fulfilling
prophesy of gloom and doom for Japan, but neither

105

do we want to avoid an important possibility. While
we encourage cooperation and interdependence in
principle and practice with Japan, we should
simultaneously be prepared for the failure of such
efforts.

Let Japan Down Gently

There has been a great deal of discussion in
recent years about fitting Japan equitably into the
dominant triangular relationship in international
affairs.[11] The Japanese themselves are in a quandary
about how to approach the issue. Although Japan's
leaders now generally look outward to broader international vistas, their people basically still look
inward. In addition, the Japanese are faced with
the underlying problem related to their prospective
larger role. That would be role largely grew out of
Japan's economic prowess. Yet, while Western states
seem willing to grant greater international stature
solely on the basis of Japan's admittedly vulnerable
economy, other states -- notably the communist
states and the resource-rich but less developed
states -- are not as favorably disposed. The Soviet
Union, in particular, does not accept economic
strength as a sufficient criterion upon which to
claim power.[12] Recognizing that their economic
"feet of clay" could not forever remain concealed,
the Japanese government's official statements on
the strategic situation of the 1970s reflected a
sophisticated awareness of the different qualities
of power.[13]

Were the Japanese economy not as fragilely
dependent on outside supports, the Japanese position
among those on the multi-polaric fringes of power

might be more secure. However, their future is too
tenuous to warrant a sense of security. The Japanese
with their fragile economic "strength" have not been
well received by others who possess stronger claims
to a place on the second level of power. Japan's
weak claim to the fringe of power presents dangers.
The reasons for Japan's essential weakness are not
well understood abroad or within Japan. Japan's
economy appears strong and vibrant and in present
day narrowly economic terms its appearance is
accurate. However, in long-run terms, the terms used
by strategists and those utilizing a neo-Malthusian
perspective, Japan's economy and hence its claim to
power are excessively vulnerable. The difficulty is
that not many people view Japan in the latter terms
yet and they may not do so until and unless Japan
begins to falter. In the intervening time, and at
present, it is too easy for both Japanese and non-
Japanese to misunderstand the reasons behind any
hesitancy to grant Japan the international stature
it apparently deserves. As the only non-Western
entry in a game of high economic and political
stakes, the Japanese have been extremely sensitive
to racial and cultural slights. Unless they fully
comprehend the reasons for their less than total
acceptance as a national power, there is serious
danger that they might misconstrue their rejection
as ethnically inspired. The added difficulty with
this prospect is that there is unquestionably some
validity to Japanese suspicions. Because of that
modicum of truth it may be doubly difficult to
disabuse the Japanese of such a notion.

Whether for reasons of strategic ineligibility or for misconstrued rejection, the Japanese appear likely to be repeatedly rebuffed in their sometimes floundering quest for some degree of added international stature befitting their economic world-rank. Despite the fact that the Japanese originally were rather unenthusiastic about assuming a larger political role, they have largely been convinced that some such role is now their due. By now the Japanese believe they are full fledged members of the "club" of advanced industrial democracies -- entitled to all the perquisites of membership. In a sense they are correct, but in a more meaningful sense they have been misled. This too creates difficulties for -- as many authorities on Japanese culture have observed -- the Japanese sense of honor and the consequences likely to follow any violation of their honor are critical considerations when dealing with the Japanese.[14] If the Japanese are to be disappointed in their inflated expectations or idealistic hopes, it would be wise for all concerned to let them down gently.

Gradual Estrangement

Letting the Japanese down gently implies varying degrees of estrangement in Japan's relations with its current trade partners. As long as this process does not lead to perversely expanded ties to countries such as the Soviet Union or the People's Republic of China which might be detrimental to the interests of Japan's current allies and friends, there is not any inherent reason to fear a gradual loosening of the bonds.

108

For the present there is little necessity for
Japan's partners in interdependence to hedge their
policies out of fear of Japan's vulnerabilities.
Indeed, if anything, their policies in support of
cooperation with Japan should be strengthened to
help fend off possible disaster. Strong support for
what was described here as utopian levels of international cooperation is likely to prove essential
not only for Japan's economic well being but for the
very long term viability of the entire international
community. On the other hand, looking much further
down the road at the possibility that cooperation
may well fail, by encouraging Japan's gradual
diversification within a bond of interdependence
Japan's trade partners will be taking the first
tentative steps toward the loosening of bilateral
ties with Japan which could be required in their
own national interests should Japan be confronted
by and unable to cope with a global economy showing
signs of slipping over the edge of the Malthusian
abyss.

NOTES

1. Yoshida, Shigeru, Japan's Decisive Century, 1867-
1967 (New York, 1967), p. 110.

2. The former foreign minister and probable future
prime minister was quoted in John K. Emmerson, Arms,
Yen & Power, The Japanese Dilemma (New York, 1971),
pp. 378-379.

3. Satō, Eisaku, New Tasks for Japan (Tokyo, 1969),
p. 13; and Kajima Morinosuke, Modern Japan's Foreign
Policy (Tokyo, 1969), p. 129.

4. Yoshida, Shigeru, The Yoshida Memoirs (London, 1961), p. 96.

5. The U.S.-Japan Trade Council's Report No. 20, Japan's Policy on Primary Commodities, p. 5, 1976, lists the following rates of Japanese dependency on Less Developed Countries:

Commodity	Dependence on LDCs
Wheat	0.4%
Grains	20
Sugar	46
Coffee	100
Cocoa	100
Tea	13
Rubber	100
Raw Cotton	67
Jute	100
Wool	3
Copper	44
Tin	97
Lead	26
Zinc	47
Bauxite	44
Iron and ore	46

Japan's trade with less developed nations will depend in part upon its ability to provide economic assistance to these countries. For a review of Japan's overseas assistance programs, see the summary of Japan's 1975 White Paper on Economic Cooperation in the Japan Trade Center report NR-83, January 1976.

6. See the 1975, 1976, and 1977 Economic Planning Angency White Papers. Summaries of these papers are available in Fall issues of Focus Japan for each

year. In addition to these official evaluations, there are private economic research facilities in Japan which produce important studies of interest to readers. Prominent facilities include: Japan Economic Research Center (JERC) the most famous; Research Institute for the National Economy (RINE); Nikko Research Center; Kyoto University Economic Research Center; The Industrial Bank of Japan; Bank of Tokyo; Daiwa Securities, Research Department; Mitsubishi Bank; Nihon Keizai Shimbun; Keidanren; Yamaichi Securities, Economic Research Institute; Nomura Research Institute; Sumitomo Bank; Mitsubishi Research Institute; Electric Power Industry Research Institute; Saitama Bank; Fuji Bank; Tokai Bank; Mitsui Bank; and Nikkei Economic Electronic Data-bank Services (NEEDS).

7. U.S.-Japan Trade Council's Report No. 32, Japan's New Economic Plan: Toward a Stabilized Society, 1976.

8. Though the relatively resource-rich nations may scoff at this notion, for the resource-poor states it is a critically important way to view the future of international relations. However, for the resource-rich as well, the day will come when the well will run dry if they do not take preventative measures. Consequently it is equally vital for their long-term interests that global cooperation of utopian proportions succeed. Though the author sincerely hopes that such "utopianism" will become the reality of future generations, doubts about mankind's brotherly instincts compels him to be pessimistic about that prospect.

9. For a discussion of the inevitable conflicts which will arise as mankind's growing numbers seek

to share access to a global "commons" see Garrett
Hardin, "The survival of nations and civilizations"
in Science, 6/25/71, p. 1297.

10. In the postwar period some of the most national-
istic voices emanating from Japan ironically have
been from the Left. Calls for an independent and
autonomous stance in foreign policy, for a halt to
Japan's subservient international posture, have come
not from the mainstream conservatives but from the
Left. The miniscule group of fanatical right-wingers
have, indeed, weakly echoed the Left, but they are
too insignificant to count in the final tally.
Japan's socialists and communists heretofore were
not able to capitalize on the negative attributes
of late-blooming industrializing societies. Much of
the political virtues of aiding the process of social and economic modernization were already the
possession of the established revolutionaries of
the Meiji period. The latter group had already laid
claim to being the only authentic revolutionary
nationalists, thereby usurping the title and denying
Japan's leftists a rallying point which enabled
left-wing nationalists to succeed elsewhere in Asia.
However, in the postwar period the Left has been
able to oust the conservatives from their proprie-
tary claims upon nationalism. Seen in a future
ecopolitical context of extreme environmental
constraints, Japanese center-left nationalism has
the potential to become dominant and to lead the
way in seeking reliable access to needed resources
among other left-nationalist states.

11. For example see, Herman Kahn, The Emerging
Japanese Superstate (Englewood Cliffs, 1970),

pp. 180-181, who questions not whether but how it will occur. In contrast, Robert Scalapino, United States & Japan: Danger Ahead (Washington, 1971), p. 10, doubts that Japan realistically can be included.

12. This is ironic since the Soviet's Marxist schema emphasizes the role of economics. Nevertheless, for the Soviet Union political power equates primarily with armed force.

13. Japanese Defense Agency, Defense White Papers (Tokyo, 1970, 1976, 1977).

14. For assessments of the role of honor in Japan, see: Ruth Benedict, The Chrysanthemum and the Sword (New York, 1946), p. 171; and Nitobe Inazo, Bushido, The Soul of Japan (New York, 1905), p. 137.

BIBLIOGRAPHY

JAPAN-RELATED

Ackerman, Edward A.. Japan's Natural Resources and
    Their Relation to Japan's Economic Future.
    Chicago: The University of Chicago Press, 1953.
Akutagawa, Ryūnosuke. Kappa. Tokyo: The Hokuseido
    Press, 1949.
Anesaki, Masaharu. Art, Life, and Nature in Japan.
    Westport: Greenwood Press, 1971 (Reprint of
    Boston: Marshal Jones Company, Inc., 1933).
Aono, Tadao. Kigyō to Kankyō (Business and the Envi-
    ronment). Tokyo: Sangyo Noritsu Tankidaigaku
    Shuppanbu, 1971.
Asahi Shimbun Correspondents (compilers). 28 Years
    in the Guam Jungle. Tokyo: Japan Publications,
    Inc., 1972.
Bellah, Robert N.. Tokugawa Religion: the Values of
    Pre-industrial Japan. Glencoe: The Free Press,
    1957.
Benedict, Ruth. The Chrysanthemum and the Sword.
    New York: Houghton Mifflin & Co., 1946.
Bisson, T.A.. Shadow Over Asia, The Rise of Militant
    Japan. New York: The Foreign Policy Association,
    Inc., 1941.

114

Brzezinski, Zbigniew. "Japan's Global Engagement" in
Foreign Affairs, January 1972, pp. 270-282.

Burks, Ardath W.. The Government of Japan. New York:
Thomas Y. Crowell Company, 1964.

Clark, Gregory. "The fragile face of force" in
Survival, March 1970, pp. 85-89.

Colgrove, Kenneth W.. Militarism in Japan. Boston:
World Peace Foundation, 1936.

Conolly, Violet. "Soviet-Japanese economic cooperation in Siberia" in The Pacific Community,
October 1970, pp. 55-65.

"Consumerism" in Japan Quarterly, July-September,
1973, pp. 255-258.

Crocker, Walter R.. The Japanese Population Problem,
The Coming Crisis. London: George Allen &
Unwin, Ltd., 1931.

Danno, Nobuo. "The changing face of agriculture" in
Japan Quarterly, July-September 1972, pp. 292-
300.

Dator, James A.. "The Protestant ethic in Japan" in
George K. Yamamoto and Ishida Tsuyoshi, (eds.).
Modern Japanese Society. Berkeley: McCutchan
Publishing Co., 1971.

Defense of Japan (Defense White Papers). Tokyo:
Japan Defense Agency, 1970, 1976, and 1977.

DeMente, Boye and Fred T. Perry. The Japanese as
Consumers. Tokyo: John Weatherhill, Inc., 1967.

Dimock, Marshall E.. The Japanese Technocracy. New
York and Tokyo: Walker/Weatherhill, 1968.

Dore, Ronald P.. "Japan as a model of economic
development" in Archives européennes de sociologie, 1964, pp. 138-154.

Dore, Ronald P.. Land Reform in Japan. London:
Oxford University Press, 1959.

115

Dunn, C.J.. Everyday Life in Traditional Japan. New York: G.P. Putnam's Sons, 1969.

Economic Planning for the Second Half of the 1970s. Tokyo: Economic Planning Agency, 1976.

Emmerson, John K.. Arms, Yen & Power, The Japanese Dilemma. New York: Dunellen Publishing Co., 1971.

Environmental Pollution and Japanese Industry. Tokyo: Keidanren, 1973 and 1975.

Environmental Protection in Tokyo. Tokyo: Tokyo Metropolitan Research Institute for Environmental Protection, 1970.

Fisher, Charles A.. "The expansion of Japan: a study in Oriental geopolitics" in Geographical Journal, Vol. 115, 1950, pp. 1-19, 179-193.

Fujiwara, Hirotatsu. "Nationalism and the ultraright wing" in Annals of the Academy of Political and Social Science, November 1956.

Fukui, Haruhiro. "Economic planning in postwar Japan: a case study in policy making" in Asian Survey, April 1972, pp. 327-348.

Fukutake, Tadashi. Asian Rural Society: China, India, Japan. Seattle: University of Washington Press, 1967.

Fukutake, Tadashi. Japanese Rural Society. New York: Oxford University Press, 1967.

Fukutake, Tadashi. Man and Society in Japan. Tokyo: University of Tokyo Press, 1962.

Gleason, Alan H.. "Economic growth and consumption in Japan" in William W. Lockwood (ed.). The State and Economic Enterprise in Japan. Princeton: Princeton University Press, 1965.

Goldman, Marshall I.. "Environmental disruption in Japan: again the Japanese outdo us" in Marshall

116

I. Goldman, (ed.). Ecology and Economics:
Controlling Pollution in the 70s. Englewood
Cliffs: Prentice-Hall, Inc., 1972.

Gotō, Kunio. Bunmei, Gijutsu, Ningen (Culture, Technology, Man). Kyoto: Hōritsu Bunkasha, 1972.

Gulick, Sidney L.. The East and The West, A Study of
Their Psychic and Cultural Characteristics.
Tokyo: Charles E. Tuttle Company, 1963.

Hall, Robert B.. Japan: Industrial Power of Asia.
Princeton: Van Nostrand, 1963.

Hauser, Philip M., (ed.). Urbanization in Asia and
the Far East. Calcutta UNESCO, 1957.

Hellman, Donald C.. Japan and East Asia: The New
International Order. New York: Praeger Publishers, 1972.

Hewes, Laurence I., Jr.. Japan -- Land and Man, An
Account of the Japanese Land Reform Program --
1945-51. Ames: The Iowa State College Press,
1955.

Hibino, Kazuyuki. "Tokyo: the overpopulated megalo-
polis" in Japan Quarterly, April-June 1973, pp.
203-212.

Hitchcock, David I.. "Joint development of Siberia:
decision-making in Japanese-Soviet relations"
in Asian Survey, March 1971, pp. 279-300.

Hoshino, Yoshirō. Hankōgai no Ronri (Logic of Anti-
pollution). Tokyo: Keisō Shobō, 1972.

Hoshino, Yoshirō. "Remodeling the archipelago" in
Japan Quarterly, January-March 1973, pp. 39-45.

Hout, Thomas. Japan's Trade Policy and U.S. Trade
Performance. New York: The Boston Consulting
Group, issued through the Japan Information
Service, Consulate General of Japan, 1973.

Hubbard, G.E.. Eastern Industrialization and its
    Effect on the West. London: Oxford University
    Press, 1938.

Hunsberger, Warren S.. Japan, New Industrial Giant.
    New York: American-Sian Educational Exchange/
    National Strategy Information Center, 1972.

Inouye, Kaoru. "L'économie japonaise d'après-guerre:
    perspective et retrospective" in Asie nouvelle,
    November-December, 1964, pp. 9-13.

Ishida Ryujiro. Geography of Japan. Tokyo: Kokusai
    Bunka Shinkōkai, 1961.

Ishii, Ryōichi. Population Pressure and Economic Life
    in Japan. London: P.S. King & Son, Ltd., 1937.

Itagaki, Yōichi. Nihon no Shigen Mondai (Resource
    Problems of Japan). Tokyo: Nihon Keizai Shim-
    bunsha, 1972.

Jacobs, Norman. The Origin of Modern Capitalism and
    Eastern Asia. Hong Kong: Hong Kong University
    Press, 1958.

Jansen, Marius B.. "Changing Japanese attitudes
    toward modernization" in Marius B. Jansen, (ed.)
    Changing Japanese Attitudes Toward Modernization.
    Princeton: Princeton University Press, 1965.

Jansen, Marius B.. "Ultranationalism in post-war
    Japan" in The Political Quarterly, April-June
    1956.

Japan, America's Largest Overseas Farm Market.
    Washington: U.S.-Japan Trade Council, 1973.

Japan Institute of International Affairs. White
    Papers of Japan, 1970-71. Tokyo: East West
    Publications, 1972.

Japan in the United Nations. Tokyo: Public Affairs
    Bureau, Ministry of Foreign Affairs, 1969.

118

Japan's Industrial Role in Overseas Cooperation for
      Development. Tokyo: Asahi Shimbunsha, 1969.
Japan's New Economic Plan: Toward a Stabilized
      Society. Washington: U.S.-Japan Trade Council,
      1976.
Japan's Overseas Private Investment -- Growth and
      Change. Washington: U.S. Department of State,
      1973.
Japan's Policy on Primary Commodities. Washington:
      U.S.-Japan Trade Council, 1976.
Kahn, Herman. The Emerging Japanese Superstate.
      Englewood Cliffs: Prentice-Hall, Inc., 1970.
Kaji, Kōji. Kōgai Gyōsei no Sōtenken (Total Review
      of Pollution Administration). Tokyo: Kōdō
      Shuppan, 1971.
Kajima, Morinosuke. Modern Japan's Foreign Policy.
      Tokyo: Charles E. Tuttle, Publishers, 1969.
Kankyō Hōrei Kenkyukai (Environmental Law Research
      Society). Kōgai Gairon (Pollution Outline).
      Tokyo: Zeimu Keiri Kyōkai, 1972.
Katō, Tadoru. Kōgai no Miraizō (The Future of Pollu-
      tion). Tokyo: Nihon Seisanbu Honbu, 1970.
Kawasaki, Ichirō. Japan Unmasked. Tokyo: Charles E.
      Tuttle Company, 1969.
Keene, Donald (ed.). Modern Japanese Literature.
      New York: Grove Press, Inc., 1956.
Keizai Shingikai Shigen Kenkyū Iinkai (Economic
      Review Society, Resource Research Committee).
      Kokusaika Jidai no Shigen Mondai (Resource
      Problems of an Internationalized Period).
      Tokyo: Okurashō Insatsukyoku, 1970.
Kishida, Junnosuke. "New problems of advanced
      societies" in Japan Quarterly, April- June
      1973, pp. 176-182.

Kitagawa, Joseph M.. "Religious & cultural ethos of
      modern Japan" in George K. Yamamoto and Ishida
      Tsuyoshi (eds.). Modern Japanese Society.
      Berkeley: McCutchan Publishing Co., 1971.

Kōgai Benran (Handbook on Environmental Pollution).
      Tokyo: Nihon Sōgō Shuppan Kikō, 1972.

Krotov, V.A., et. al.. "The role of eastern Siberia
      in solving some of the economic problems of the
      Pacific basin" in Soviet Geography, February
      1968, pp. 142-144.

Kunimoto, Yoshirō. "Deserted mountain villages of
      western Japan" in Japan Quarterly, January-
      March 1973, pp. 87-96.

Lasswell, Harold D.. "Religion and modernization in
      the Far East" in Far Eastern Quarterly, Vol. 12,
      1953, pp. 123-202.

Levy, Walter J.. "An Atlantic-Japanese energy
      policy" in Foreign Policy, Summer 1973, pp.
      159-190.

Livermore, Arthur H., (ed.). Science in Japan.
      Washington: American Association for the
      Advancement of Science, 1965.

Lockwood, William W.. The Economic Development of
      Japan: Growth and Structural Change, 1868-1938.
      Princeton: Princeton University Press, 1954.

Lory, Hillis. Japan's Military Masters. New York:
      The Viking Press, 1943.

Maruyama, Masao. Thought and Behavior in Modern
      Japan. Cambridge: Harvard University Press,
      1969.

Matsumoto, Shōetsu. Kōgai to Kihonteki Jinken
      (Public Hazards and Fundamental Human Rights).
      Tokyo: Keibundō, 1972.

Mitsubishi Miraikan, Nihon no Shizen to Nihonjin no
    Yume (The Mitsubishi Future Hall, Nature in
    Japan and the Dreams of the Japanese). Prepared
    for Mitsubishi's exhibit at Osaka's Expo '70,
    undated.

Miyamoto Mataji, Sakudō Yōtarō, and Yasuba Yasukichi.
    "Economic development in pre-industrial Japan,
    1859-1894" in Journal of Economic History,
    December 1965, pp. 541-564.

Moore, Charles A. (ed.). The Japanese Mind, Essen-
    tials of Japanese Philosophy and Culture.
    Honolulu: East-West Center Press, 1967.

✓ Morley, James W.. "Growth for what? the issue of the
    seventies" in Gerald L. Curtis (ed.). Japanese-
    American Relations in the 1970s. Washington:
    Columbia Books, Inc., 1970.

Morris, Ivan (ed.). Japan 1931-1945, Militarism,
    Fascism, Japanism?. Boston: D.C. Heath and
    Company, 1963.

Morris, Ivan. "Significance of the military in post-
    war Japan" in Pacific Affairs, March 1958.

Moulton, Harold G. and Louis Marlio. The Control of
    Germany and Japan. Washington: The Brookings
    Institution, 1944.

Muraoka, Tsunetsugu. Studies in Shinto Thought.
    Tokyo: UNESCO and Ministry of Education, 1964.

Nakane, Chie. Japanese Society. Berkeley: University
    of California Press, 1970.

Nakayama, Ichirō. Industrialization of Japan. Tokyo:
    The Centre for East Asian Cultural Studies,
    1963.

Nihonkan, Nihon to Nihonjin (Japanese Pavilion,
    Japan and the Japanese). Osaka: Tsūsho Sangyō-
    shō, Nihon Bōeki Shinkokai, undated; ca. 1970.

121

<u>Nihon Rettō Kaizōron Hihan</u> (Criticism on the Theory
    of Remodeling the Japanese Archipelago). Tokyo:
    Yomiuri Shimbunsha, 1972.

Nishibori, Masahiro. <u>Japan Views the United Nations</u>.
    Tokyo: Ministry of Foreign Affairs, 1970.

Nitobe, Inazo. <u>Bushido, The Soul of Japan</u>. Tokyo:
    Charles E. Tuttle, 1969 (Originally published,
    New York: G.P. Putnam's Sons, 1905).

Northrop, Filmer S.C.. <u>The Meeting of East and West</u>.
    New York: The Macmillan Company, 1946.

Numata, Jirō. "The acceptance of Western culture in
    Japan" in <u>Monumenta Nipponica</u>, Vol. 19, 1964,
    pp. 1-8.

Ogura, T. (ed.). <u>Agricultural Development in Modern
    Japan</u>. Tokyo: Fuji Publishing Co., Ltd., 1963.

Okawa, Kazushi, Bruce F. Johnston, and Kaneda Hiro-
    mitsu (eds.). <u>Agriculture and Economic Growth:
    Japan's Experience</u>. Princeton: Princeton Uni-
    versity Press, 1970.

Okita, Saburō. "Japan and the world economy through
    the 1970s: a projection" in <u>Japan Report</u>
    (Special Supplement), 7/16/72, pp. 1-16.

Ōmori, Shigeo. "Two tasks for Tanaka" in <u>Japan
    Quarterly</u>, October-December 1972, pp. 403-414.

Penrose, Ernest F.. <u>Food Supply and Raw Materials in
    Japan, 1894-1927</u>. Chicago: University of
    Chicago Press, 1930.

"Pollution case law" in <u>Japan Quarterly</u>, July-
    September 1973, pp. 251-254.

Pond, Elizabeth. "Japan and Russia: the view from
    Tokyo" in <u>Foreign Affairs</u>, October 1973, pp.
    141-152.

<u>Problems of the Human Environment in Japan</u>. Tokyo:
    Ministry of Foreign Affairs, 1971.

Quigg, Philip W.. "Japan in neutral" in Foreign
    Affairs, January 1966.
Richardson, Bradley M.. The Political Culture of
    Japan. Berkeley: University of California Press,
    1973.
Rosovsky, Henry. "Japan's economic future" in
    Challenge, July-August, 1973, pp. 6-17.
Saeki, Kiichi. "Toward Japanese cooperation in
    Siberian development" in Problems of Communism,
    May-June 1972, pp. 1-11.
Sakamaki, Shunzō. "Shintō: Japanese ethnocentrism"
    in Charles A. Moore (ed.). The Japanese Mind,
    Essentials of Japanese Philosophy and Culture.
    Honolulu: East-West Center Press, 1967.
Sansom, George B.. The Western World and Japan, A
    Study in the Interaction of European and
    Asiatic Cultures. New York: Alfred A. Knopf,
    1950.
Satō, Eisaku. New Tasks for Japan. Tokyo: Ministry
    of Foreign Affairs, 1969.
Sebald, William J. and C. Nelson Spinks. Japan:
    Prospects, Options, and Opportunites. Washing-
    ton: American Enterprise Institute for Public
    Policy Research, 1967.
Shand, R.T. (ed.). Agricultural Development in Asia.
    Berkeley: University of California Press, 1969.
Smith, Peter. "Japan: economic dream, ecological
    nightmare" in Ecologist, December 1971, pp.
    16-19.
Smith, Thomas C.. The Agrarian Origins of Modern
    Japan. Stanford: Stanford University Press,
    1959.
Smith, Thomas C.. "Introduction of Western industry
    to Japan during the last years of the Tokugawa

period" in Harvard Journal of Asiatic Studies,
No. 11, 1948, pp. 130-152.

Spencer, Robert F. (ed.). Religion and Change in
Contemporary Asia. Minneapolis: University of
Minnesota Press, 1971.

Stone, Peter B.. Japan Surges Ahead, Japan's Economic Rebirth. London: Weidenfeld & Nicolson, 1969.

Storry, Richard. "Japanese attitudes to the West" in
Raghaven Iyer (ed.). The Glass Curtain Between
Asia and Europe. London: Oxford University
Press, 1965.

Taeuber, Irene B.. "Japan's population: miracle,
model, or case study" in Foreign Affairs, Vol.
40, 1962, pp. 595-604.

Taeuber, Irene B.. The Population of Japan. Princeton: Princeton University Press, 1958.

Taira, Koji. "Power and trade in U.S.-Japanese relations" in Asian Survey, November 1972, pp. 980-
998.

Takai, Fuyuji, Matsumoto Tatsurō, and Toriyama
Ryūzō. Geology of Japan. Berkeley: University
of California Press, 1963.

Takeshita, John T.. "Population control in Japan: a
miracle or secular trend" in George K. Yamamoto
and Ishida Tsuyoshi (eds.). Modern Japanese
Society. Berkeley: McCutchan Publishing Co.,
1971.

Taketani, Mitsuo. Kōgai Anzensei Jinken (Safeguarding Human Rights from Pollution). Tokyo:
Yomiuri Shimbunsha, 1972.

Tanaka, Kakuei. Nihon Rettō Kaizōron (Remodeling the
Japanese Archipelago). Tokyo: Okurasho, 1971.

Tomono, Rihei. Kōgai Yōgojiten (Glossary of Environmental Pollution). Tokyo: Omusha, 1973.

Tōyama, Shigeki. "Politics, economics, and the international environment in the Meiji and Taisho periods" in Developing Economies, December 1966, pp. 419-446.

Trewartha, Glenn T.. Japan, A Geography. Madison: University of Wisconsin Press, 1965.

Tsunoda, Ryusaku, Wm. Theodore DeBary, and Donald Keene. Sources of Japanese Tradition. New York: Columbia University Press, 1964.

Uemura, Kogorō. "Contribution to world economic prosperity and the course of Japanese economy" in Keidanren Review, Summer 1971, pp. 2-4.

Ui, Jun. Kōgai Rettō, 70 Nendai (Pollution Archipelago, the 1970s). Tokyo: Akishobō, 1972.

✓ Ui, Jun. The singularities of Japanese pollution" in Japan Quarterly, July-September 1972, pp. 281-291.

Unger, Jonathan. "Japan: the economic threat" in Survival, January-February 1972, pp. 38-42.

United States & Japan, Danger Ahead. Washington: U.S.-Japan Trade Council, 1971.

Japanese Attitudes on Important Economic Issues. Washington: U.S.I.A., Office of Research, 1974.

Urano, Tatsuo. Gendai Kokusai Seiji no Kadai (Issues of Modern International Politics). Tokyo: Yūshindō, 1970.

Vogel, Ezra F.. Japan's New Middle Class. Berkeley: University of California Press, 1967.

Wakaizumi, Kei. "Japan's role in a new world order" in Foreign Affairs, January 1973, pp. 310-326.

Ward, Robert E.. "Japan: the continuity of modernization" in Lucien W. Pye and Sidney Verba. Political Culture and Political Development. Princeton: Princeton University Press, 1965.

Weinstein, Martin E.. Japan's Postwar Defense Policy.
New York: Columbia University Press, 1971.

Wohlstetter, Albert. "Japan's security: balancing
after the shocks" in Foreign Affairs, Winter
1972-73, pp. 171-190.

Yamamura, Kōzō. "Growth vs economic democracy in
Japan: 1945-1965" in Journal of Asian Studies
August 1966, pp. 713-728.

Yazaki, Takeo. Social Change and the City in Japan.
Tokyo: Japan Publications, Inc., 1968.

Yoshida, Shigeru. Japan's Decisive Century, 1867-
1967. New York: Frederick A. Praeger, 1967.

Yoshida, Shigeru. The Yoshida Memoirs. London:
William Heinemann, Ltd., 1961.

Yoshida, Toshio. Nihon no Shizen (Nature of Japan).
Tokyo: Kōyōshoin, 1968.

GENERAL

"Asian population explosion" in Japan Quarterly,
April-June 1973, pp. 138-142.

Bates, Marston. The Forest and the Sea: A Look at
the Economy of Nature and the Ecology of Man.
New York: Random House, 1960.

Bates, Marston. Man in Nature. Englewood Cliffs:
Prentice-Hall, Inc., 1964.

Baudet, Henri. Paradise on Earth, Some Thought on
European Images of Non-European Man. New Haven:
Yale University Press, 1965.

Black, John. The Dominion of Man: The Search for
Ecological Responsibility. Edinburgh: Edinburgh
University Press, 1970.

"Blueprint for Survival" in Ecologist, January 1972, pp. 1-43.

Borgstrom, Georg. The Hungry Planet. New York: The Macmillan Company, 1965.

Boulding, Kenneth E.. "Fun and games with the Gross National Product - the role of misleading indicators in social policy" in Harold W. Helfrich, Jr., (ed.). The Environmental Crisis, Man's Struggle to Live with Himself. New Haven: Yale University Press, 1970.

Boyle, Thomas J.. "Hope for the technological solution" in Nature, 9/21/73, pp. 127-128.

Bronwell, Arthur B. (ed.). Science and Technology in the World of the Future. New York: John Wiley & Sons, Inc., 1970.

Brown, Harrison. The Challenge of Man's Future. New York: The Viking Press, 1954.

Brown, Lester R.. "The agricultural revolution in Asia" in Foreign Affairs, July 1968.

Brown, Lester R.. "Scarce food: here to stay" in Washington Post, 7/15/73, pp. C1 and C4.

Brown, Lester R.. Seeds of Change: The Green Revolution and Development in the 1970s. New York: Praeger Publishers, 1970.

Brown, Lester R.. "The world outlook for conventional agriculture" in Science, 11/7/67.

Brubaker, Sterling. To Live On Earth. Baltimore: Resources for the Future, Inc. and The Johns Hopkins Press, 1972.

Calder, Ritchie. How Long Have We Got?. Montreal: McGill-Queen's University Press, 1972.

Caldwell, Lynton K.. Environment: A Challenge for Modern Society. Garden City, NY: American Museum of Natural History, 1970.

Caldwell, Mary Ellen. "Population" in Cyril E. Black
and Richard A. Falk, (eds.). The Future of the
International Legal Order, The Structure of the
International Environment. Princeton: Princeton
University Press, 1972.

Carpenter, J. Henry. Peace Through Cooperation. New
York: Harper & Brothers, 1944.

Carson, Rachel. Silent Spring. New York: Fawcett
Publications, Inc., 1970.

Castro, Josué de. The Geography of Hunger. Boston:
Little, Brown and Company, 1952.

Ciriacy-Wantrup, S.V. and James J. Parsons. Natural
Resources: Quality and Quantity. Berkeley:
University of California Press, 1967.

Clark, Colin. "Population growth and living stand-
ards" in A.N. Agarwala and S.P. Singh, (eds.).
The Economic of Underdevelopment. London:
Oxford University Press, 1958.

Clark, Collin. "World power and population" in Walt
Anderson (ed.). Politics and Environment.
Pacific Palisades: Goodyear Publishing Co.,
1970.

Clemens, Walter C., Jr.. "Ecology & International
Relations" in International Journal, Winter
1972-73, pp. 1-27.

Club of Rome. "The Club of Rome answers its critics
and pushes on" in War/Peace Report, May-June
1973, pp. 21-29.

Collingwood, Francis J.. Philosophy of Nature.
Englewood Cliffs: Prentice-Hall, 1961.

Collingwood, R.G.. The Idea of Nature. New York:
Oxford University Press, 1945.

Commoner, Barry. The Closing Circle, Nature, Man,
and Technology. New York: Alfred A. Knopf, 1972.

Commoner, Barry. Science and Survival. New York:
    Viking Press, 1966.
Conway, Mimi. "Asia: the unnatural rape" in Far
    Eastern Economic Review, 4/23/70, pp. 21-31.
Coontz, Sydney H.. Population Theories and the
    Economic Interpretation. London: Routledge &
    Kegan Paul, Ltd., 1957.
Dahlberg, Kenneth A.. "The technological ethic and
    the spirit of international relations" in Inter-
    national Studies Quarterly, March 1973, pp. 55-
    88.
Detwyler, Thomas R.. Man's Impact on the Environment.
    New York: McGraw-Hill Book Co., 1971.
Dorn, Harold F.. "World population growth" in Philip
    M. Hauser, (ed.). The Population Dilemma. Engle-
    wood Cliffs: Prentice-Hall, 1963.
Dorst, Jean. Before Nature Dies. New York: Houghton
    Mifflin Co., 1970.
Dubos, Rene. So Human an Animal. New York: Charles
    Scribner's Sons, 1969.
Editors of Ramparts. Eco-Catastrophe. New York:
    Harper & Row, Publishers, 1970.
Ehrlich, Paul R.. "Famine 1975: fact or fallacy" in
    Harold W. Helrich, Jr. (ed.). The Environmental
    Crisis, Man's Struggle to Live with Himself.
    New Haven: Yale University Press, 1970.
Ehrlich, Paul R.. The Population Bomb. New York:
    Ballantine Books, 1968.
Ehrlich, Paul R. & Anne H. Ehrlich. Population,
    Resources, Environment. San Francisco: W.H.
    Freeman and Co., 1970.
Ellul, Jacques. Technological Society. New York:
    Alfred A. Knopf, 1964

Eyre, S.R. and G.R.J. Jones. Geography as Human
    Ecology. London: Edward Arnold, Ltd., 1966.

Falk, Richard A.. "Environmental policy as a world
    order problem" in Natural Resources Journal,
    April 1972, pp. 161-171.

Falk, Richard A.. "Toward a world order respectful
    of the global ecosystem" in Environmental
    Affairs, June 1971, pp. 251-265.

Farmer, Richard, John D. Long and George J. Stolnitz.
    World Population: The View Ahead. Bloomington:
    Indiana University Press, 1971.

Farvar, M. Taghi. "The pollution of Asia" in Environ-
    ment, October 1971, pp. 10-17.

Fisher, Joseph L. and Neal Potter. "Resources in the
    United States and the world" in Philip Hauser,
    (ed.). The Population Dilemma. Englewood Cliffs:
    Prentice-Hall, Inc., 1963.

Freeman, Christopher. "Malthus with a computer" in
    H.S.D. Cole, et. al.. Models of Doom, A Criti-
    que of The Limits to Growth. New York: Universe
    Books, 1973.

Geiger, Theodore. The Conflicted Relationship: The
    West and the Transformation of Asia, Africa and
    Latin America. New York: McGraw-Hill, 1967.

Georgescu-Roegen, Nicholas. The Entropy Law and the
    Economic Process. Cambridge: Havard University
    Press, 1971.

Georgescu-Roegen, Nicholas. "Energy and economic
    myths" in Southern Economic Journal, January
    1975, pp. 347-381.

Ginsberg, Norton. "Natural resources and economic
    development" in Annals of the Association of
    American Geographers, Vol. 47, No. 3, 1957,
    pp. 196-212.

Glacken, Clarence J.. "Changing ideas of the habitable world" in W.L. Thomas, Jr. (ed.). Man's Role in Changing the Face of the Earth. Chicago: University of Chicago Press, 1956.

Glacken, Clarence J.. "Man against nature: an outdated concept" in Harold W. Helfrich, Jr. (ed.). The Environmental Crisis, Man's Struggle to Live with Himself. New Haven: Yale University Press, 1970.

Glacken, Clarence J.. Traces on the Rhodian Shore. Berkeley: University of California Press, 1967.

Gottmann, Jean. The Significance of Territory. Charlottesville: University of Virginia Press, 1973.

Graham, Frank. Since Silent Spring. Boston: Houghton Mifflin Company, 1970.

Grant, James P.. "Development: the end of trickle down?" in Foreign Policy, Fall 1973, pp. 43-65.

Hamblin, Lynette. Pollution: The World Crisis. New York: Barnes and Noble, 1970.

Haskins, Caryl P.. The Scientific Revolution and World Politics. New York: Council on Foreign Relations/Harper and Row, Publishers, 1964.

Hauser, Philip. (ed.). Population and World Politics. Glencoe: The Free Press, 1958.

Heilbroner, Robert L.. "Growth and survival" in Foreign Affairs, October 1972, pp. 139-153.

Heiss, Richard L. and Noel F. McInnis (eds.). Can Man Care for the Earth?. Nashville: Abingdon Press, 1971.

Hersch, Jeanne (ed.). Birthright of Man. Paris: UNESCO, 1969.

Herz, John H.. "The territorial state revisited: reflections on the future of the nation-state"

131

in James N. Rosenau, (ed.). <u>International Poli-</u>
<u>tics and Foreign Policy</u>. New York: The Free
Press, 1969.

Holdren, John P. and Paul R. Ehrlich (eds.). <u>Global</u>
<u>Ecology/Man and the Ecosphere</u>. San Francisco:
W.H. Freeman, 1971.

Humpstone, Charles C.. "Pollution: precedent and
prospect" in <u>Foreign Affairs</u>, January 1972,
pp. 325-338.

Huxley, Julian. "Man's place and role in nature" in
Lewis G. Leary, (ed.). <u>The Unity of Knowledge</u>.
Garden City: Doubleday & Co., 1955.

The Institute of Technology. <u>Man in the Living</u>
<u>Environment</u>. Madison: University of Wisconsin
Press, 1972.

Jacks, Graham V. and Robert O. Whyte. <u>The Rape of</u>
<u>the Earth: A World Survey of Soil Erosion</u>.
London: Faber and Faber, 1939.

Jeffries, William W.. <u>Geography and National Power</u>.
Annapolis: Naval Institute Press, 1967.

Johnson, Cecil E., (ed.). <u>The Natural World, Chaos</u>
<u>and Conservation</u>. New York: McGraw-Hill Book
Co., 1972.

Kahn, Herman and B. Bruce-Biggs. <u>Things to Come,</u>
<u>Thinking About the Seventies and Eighties</u>. New
York: The Macmillan Company, 1972.

Kay, David A. and Eugene B. Skolnikoff. "International institutions and the environmental
crisis: a look ahead" in <u>International Organi-</u>
<u>zation</u>, Winter 1972, pp. 469-478.

Kaysen, Carl. "The computer that printed out
W*O*L*F* " in <u>Foreign Affairs</u>, July 1972, pp.
660-668.

Kneese, Allen V., Sidney E. Rolfe, and Joseph W.
Harned (eds.). Managing the Environment: Inter-
national Economic Cooperation for Pollution
Control. New York: Praeger Publishers, 1971.

Koren, Henry J., (ed.). Readings in the Philosophy
of Nature. Westminster: The Newman Press, 1958.

Kristoff, Ladis K.D.. "The origins and evolution of
Geopolitics" in Journal of Conflict Resolution,
March 1960, pp. 15-51.

Kroeber, Alfred L.. "Relations of environmental and
cultural factors" in Andrew P. Vayda (ed.).
Environment and Cultural Behavior. Garden City:
The Natural History Press, 1969.

Krutilla, John V.. "Some environmental effects of
economic development" in Daedalus, Vol. 96, No.
4, 1967, pp. 1058-1070.

Leiss, William. The Domination of Nature. New York:
George Braziller, 1972.

Lorenz, Konrad. On Agression. New York: Harcourt,
Brace & World, 1966.

Lorimer, Frank. "Issues of population policy" in
Philip Hauser (ed.). The Population Dilemma.
Englewood Cliffs: Prentice-Hall, 1963.

Lowenthal, David (ed.). (George Perkins Marsh's) Man
and Nature. Cambridge: Harvard University Press,
1965.

Lyons, Barrow. Tomorrow's Birthright, A Political
and Economic Interpretation of our Natural
Resources. New York: Funk & Wagnalls Company,
1955.

Mackinder, Halford J.. Democratic Ideals and Reality.
New York: W.W. Norton & Company, Inc. 1962.

Maddox, John R.. The Doomsday Syndrome. New York:
McGraw-Hill, 1972.

Malthus, Thomas R.. On Population. New York: The
     Modern Library, 1960; (Edited and introduced by
     Gertrude Himmelfarb.).

Maritain, Jacques. Philosophy of Nature. New York:
     Philosophical Library, 1951.

Mayer, Jean and T. George Harris. "Affluence: the
     fifth horseman of the apocalypse" in Psychology
     Today, January 1970, pp. 43-50 and 58.

McHale, John. The Ecological Context. New York:
     George Braziller, 1970.

Meadows, Dennis L., Donnella H. Meadows, Jørgen
     Randers, and William H. Behrens III. "A res-
     ponse to Sussex" in H.S.D. Cole, et. al..
     Models of Doom, A Critique of the Limits to
     Growth. New York: Universe Books, 1973.

Meadows, Dennis L., et. al.. The Limits to Growth.
     New York: Universe Books, 1972.

Meek, R., (ed.). Marx and Engels on the Population
     Bomb. Berkeley: The Ramparts Press, 1971.

Millis, Walter. "Permanent Peace" in Walter Millis
     (ed.). A World Without War. New York: Washing-
     ton Square Press, Inc., 1961.

Mishan, E.J.. Technology & Growth, The Price We Pay.
     New York: Praeger Publishers, 1970.

Moncrief, Lewis W.. "The cultural basis of our envi-
     ronmental crisis" in Ian G. Barbour (ed.).
     Western Man and Environmental Ethics. Reading:
     Addison-Wesley Publishing Co., 1973.

Murphey, Rhoads. "Traditionalism and colonialism:
     changing urban roles in Asia" in Journal of
     Asian Studies, November 1969, pp. 67-84.

Myrdal, Gunnar. Rich Lands and Poor. New York:
     Harper & Row, Publishers, 1957.

Nasr, Seyyed Hossein. The Encounter of Man and Nature. London: George Allen and Unwin, Ltd., 1968.

Needham, Joseph. "Human laws and laws of nature in China and the West" in Journal of the History of Ideas, Vol. 12, 1951, pp. 3-33 and 194-230.

Needham, Joseph. The Grand Titration: Science & Society in East and West. Toronto: University of Toronto Press, 1969.

Ng, Larry K.Y. and Stuart Mudd (eds.). The Population Crisis. Bloomington: Indiana University Press, 1965.

Not Man Apart (Special issue on U.N. Conference on the Human Environment in Stockholm), Vol. 2, July 1972. Published for Friends of the Earth, John Muir Institute for Environmental Studies, and the League of Conservation Voters.

Odum, Howard T.. Environment, Power, and Society. New York: John Wiley & Sons, Inc., 1971.

Ogburn, William F., (ed.). Technology and International Relations. Chicago: University of Chicago Press, 1949.

Ordway, Samuel H.. "Possible limits of raw-material consumption" in W.L. Thomas, Jr., (ed.). Man's Role in Changing the Face of the Earth. Chicago: University of Chicago Press, 1956.

Orleans, Leo A. and Richard P. Suttmeier. "The Mao ethic and environmental quality" in Science, 12/11/70, pp. 1173-1176.

Osborn, Fairfield. Our Plundered Planet. Boston: Little, Brown and Company, 1948.

Page, William. "Population forecasting" in H.S.D. Cole, et. al.. Models of Doom, A Critique of the Limits to Growth. New York: Universe Books, 1973.

Pavitt, K.L.R.. "Malthus and other economists, some
doomsdays revisited" in H.S.D. Cole, et. al..
Models of Doom, A Critique of the Limits to
Growth. New York: Universe Books, 1973.

Possony, Stefan T. and J.E. Pournelle. The Strategy
of Technology: Winning the Decisive War.
Cambridge: University Press of Cambridge, 1970.

Renner, George T., (ed.). "Resources and world
peace" in George T. Renner (ed.). Global Geography. New York: Thomas Y. Crowel Co., 1944.

Resources and Man. San Francisco: W.H. Freeman and
Company/National Academy of Sciences, 1969.

Revelle, Roger. "Technology and human environment"
in Philip O. Foss, (ed.). Politics and Ecology.
Belmont: Duxbury Press, 1972.

Ripley, S. Dillon and Helmut K. Buechner. "Ecosystem
science as a point of synthesis" in Daedalus,
Vol. 96, No. 4, 1967, pp. 1192-1199.

Scheler, Max. Man's Place in Nature. Boston: Beacon
Press, 1961.

Schmidt, Alfred. The Concept of Nature in Marx.
London: NLB, 1971 (Translation of Europaische
Verlagsanstalt edition, 1962).

Science and Technology in Asian Development. New
Delhi: UNESCO, 1968.

Sears, Paul B.. "Man, nature, and the ecological
balance" in George T. Renner (ed.). Global Geography. New York: Thomas Y. Crowell Co., 1944.

Sears, Paul B.. "The process of environmental change
by man" in W.L. Thomas, Jr., (ed.). Man's Role
in Changing the Face of the Earth. Chicago:
University of Chicago Press, 1956.

Semple, Ellen Churchill. Influences of Geographic
Environment. New York: Russell and Russell,

1968 (Reprint of Holt, Rinehart and Winston, Inc., 1911 edition.).

Skolimowski, Henryk. "Technology vs. nature" in Ecologist, February 1973, pp. 50-55.

Smith, Guy-Harold (ed.). Conservation of Natural Resources. New York: John Wiley & Sons, 1971.

Solow, Robert M.. "Is the end of the world at hand?" in Challenge, March-April 1973, pp. 39-50.

Spengler, Joseph J., (ed.). Natural Resources and Economic Growth. Washington: Resources for the Future and Social Science Research Council, 1961.

Spoeher, Alexander. "Cultural differences in the interpretation of natural resources" in W.L. Thomas, Jr., (ed.). Man's Role in Changing the Face of the Earth. Chicago: University of Chicago Press, 1956.

Sprout, Harold and Margaret. An Ecological Paradigm for the Study of International Politics. Princeton: Princeton University Press, 1968.

Sprout, Harold and Margaret. The Ecological Perspective on Human Affairs with Special Reference to International Politics. Princeton: Princeton University Press, 1965.

Sprout, Harold and Margaret. "National priorities: demands, resources, dilemmas" in World Politics Vol. 24, January 1972, pp. 293-317.

Sprout, Harold and Margaret. Toward a Politics of the Planet Earth. New York: Van Nostrand Reinhold, 1971.

Spykman, Nicholas J.. The Geography of the Peace. New York: Harcourt, Brace and Company, 1944.

Strausz-Hupe, Robert. Geopolitics, The Struggle for Space and Power. New York: G.P. Putnam, 1942.

Teilhard de Chardin, Pierre. <u>Building the Earth</u>.
    Wilkes-Barre: Dimension Books, 1965.

Thompson, Warren S.. <u>Population and Progress in the
    Far East</u>. Chicago: University of Chicago Press,
    1959.

Tuan, Yi-fu. <u>Man and Nature</u>. Washington: Association
    of American Geographers, Resource Paper No. 10,
    1971.

Ubbelohde, A.R.. <u>Man and Energy</u>. Baltimore: Penguin
    Books, 1963.

<u>United Nations Conference on the Human Environment,
    Stockholm, 5-16 June</u>. New York: United Nations
    Press Release HE/143, 1972.

Utton, Albert E. and Daniel H. Henning. <u>Environment-
    al Policy: Concepts and International Implica-
    tions</u>. New York: Praeger Publishers, 1973.

Vogt, William. <u>Road to Survival</u>. New York: William
    Sloan Associates, Inc., 1948.

Wagner, Philip L.. <u>The Human Use of the Earth</u>.
    Glencoe: The Free Press, 1960.

Ward, Barbara and Rene Dubos. <u>Only One Earth</u>. New
    York: W.W. Norton & Co., 1972.

Watson, Richard A. and Patty J.. <u>Man and Nature</u>.
    New York: Harcourt, Brace & World, 1969.

Weigert, Hans W.. <u>Generals and Geographers, The
    Twilight of Geopolitics</u>. New York: Oxford
    University Press, 1942.

White, Lynn Jr.. "The historical roots of our eco-
    logical crisis" in <u>Science</u>, 3/10/67, pp. 1203-
    1207.

Willkie, Wendell L.. <u>One World</u>. New York: Simon and
    Schuster, 1943.

Wilson, Carroll L.. <u>Man's Impact on the Global Envi-
    ronment: Assessment & Recomendation for Action</u>.

Cambridge: The MIT Press/SCEP (Study of Critical Environmental Problems), 1970.

Wilson, Thomas W., Jr.. International Environmental
Action: A Global Survey. New York: Dunellen,
Inc. & Aspen Institute of Humanistic Studies,
1971.

Wollman, Nathaniel. "The new economics of resources"
in Daedalus, Vol. 96, No. 4, 1967, pp. 1099-
1114.

Woytinsky, W.S.. "World resources in relation to
population" in Philip M. Hauser, (ed.). Population and World Politics. Glencoe: The Free
Press, 1958.

Wright, Quincy. "Modern technology and the world
order" in William F. Ogburn (ed.). Technology
and International Relations. Chicago: University
of Chicago Press, 1949.

Zimmerman, Erich W.. World Resources & Industries.
New York: Harper & Brothers, Publishers, 1951.